NATIONAL ACADEMIES | *Sciences*
Engineering
Medicine

Rise and Thrive with Science

Teaching PK–5 Science and Engineering

Nancy Kober

with contributions from Heidi Carlone,
Elizabeth A. Davis, Ximena Dominguez,
Eve Manz, and Carla Zembal-Saul

Amy Stephens and Heidi Schweingruber, Editors

Board on Science Education

Division of Behavioral and Social Sciences and Education

National Academies Press
Washington, DC

NATIONAL ACADEMIES PRESS 500 Fifth Street, NW Washington, DC 20001

This activity was supported by a contract between the National Academy of Sciences and the Carnegie Corporation of New York (G-19-57002). Any opinions, findings, conclusions, or recommendations expressed in this publication do not necessarily reflect the views of any organization or agency that provided support for the project.

International Standard Book Number-13: 978-0-309-69821-4
International Standard Book Number-10: 0-309-69821-9
Digital Object Identifier: https://doi.org/10.17226/26853

Library of Congress Control Number: 2023949739

This publication is available from the National Academies Press, 500 Fifth Street, NW, Keck 360, Washington, DC 20001; (800) 624-6242 or (202) 334-3313; http://www.nap.edu.

Suggested citation: Kober, N., Carlone, H., Davis, E.A., Dominguez, X., Manz, E., & Zembal-Saul, C. 2023. *Rise and Thrive with Science: Teaching PK–5 Science and Engineering* (A. Stephens & H. Schweingruber, Eds.). Washington, DC: The National Academies Press. https://doi.org/10.17226/26853.

The **National Academy of Sciences** was established in 1863 by an Act of Congress, signed by President Lincoln, as a private, nongovernmental institution to advise the nation on issues related to science and technology. Members are elected by their peers for outstanding contributions to research. Dr. Marcia McNutt is president.

The **National Academy of Engineering** was established in 1964 under the charter of the National Academy of Sciences to bring the practices of engineering to advising the nation. Members are elected by their peers for extraordinary contributions to engineering. Dr. John L. Anderson is president.

The **National Academy of Medicine** (formerly the Institute of Medicine) was established in 1970 under the charter of the National Academy of Sciences to advise the nation on medical and health issues. Members are elected by their peers for distinguished contributions to medicine and health. Dr. Victor J. Dzau is president.

The three Academies work together as the **National Academies of Sciences, Engineering, and Medicine** to provide independent, objective analysis and advice to the nation and conduct other activities to solve complex problems and inform public policy decisions. The National Academies also encourage education and research, recognize outstanding contributions to knowledge, and increase public understanding in matters of science, engineering, and medicine.

Learn more about the National Academies of Sciences, Engineering, and Medicine at www.nationalacademies.org.

Consensus Study Reports published by the National Academies of Sciences, Engineering, and Medicine document the evidence-based consensus on the study's statement of task by an authoring committee of experts. Reports typically include findings, conclusions, and recommendations based on information gathered by the committee and the committee's deliberations. Each report has been subjected to a rigorous and independent peer-review process and it represents the position of the National Academies on the statement of task.

Proceedings published by the National Academies of Sciences, Engineering, and Medicine chronicle the presentations and discussions at a workshop, symposium, or other event convened by the National Academies. The statements and opinions contained in proceedings are those of the participants and are not endorsed by other participants, the planning committee, or the National Academies.

Rapid Expert Consultations published by the National Academies of Sciences, Engineering, and Medicine are authored by subject-matter experts on narrowly focused topics that can be supported by a body of evidence. The discussions contained in rapid expert consultations are considered those of the authors and do not contain policy recommendations. Rapid expert consultations are reviewed by the institution before release.

For information about other products and activities of the National Academies, please visit www.nationalacademies.org/about/whatwedo.

Contents

About This Guide

Science and engineering education for children has undergone a transformation since the 2012 publication of the *Framework for K–12 Science Education: Practices, Crosscutting Concepts, and Core Ideas* by the National Academies of Sciences, Engineering, and Medicine.[1] At the center of this transformation is a vision, grounded in research and laid out in the *Framework for K–12 Science Education*, that children learn these subjects best by engaging from an early age in the kinds of practices used by real scientists and engineers. By "doing" science and engineering, children not only develop and refine their understanding of the disciplinary core ideas and crosscutting concepts (that is, concepts that connect across disciplines and the natural world) of these disciplines, but can also be empowered to use their growing understanding to make sense of questions and problems relevant to them. This approach can make learning more meaningful, equitable, and lasting.

Many states have embraced this vision of learning by adopting the Next Generation Science Standards (NGSS) or similar state standards based on the *Framework for K–12 Science Education*. Across the country, districts and schools have been implementing their standards and transforming science and engineering instruction. To translate this vision into changes in instructional practices, educators, district and state leaders, researchers, and companies have worked intensively on curriculum development, instructional design, and classroom-focused research. These efforts have yielded a robust base of knowledge about how children learn science and engineering and an array of strategies for teaching these subjects well.

What do teachers of preschool and elementary children need?

Much of the present research, curricula, and instructional work in science and engineering education has focused on middle and high schools. Fewer resources are

---

[1] National Research Council. (2012). *A framework for K–12 science education: Practices, crosscutting concepts, and core ideas.* The National Academies Press. https://doi.org/10.17226/13165

available for educators of children in preschool through grade 5. Yet, practitioners at these levels have an immediate need for examples of classroom practice, professional development, and other supports to help them implement high-quality strategies for teaching and learning in science and engineering. Although there are thousands of instructional activities and lessons online that purport to be aligned with particular sets of standards, teachers may wonder how effective these activities are and how well they fit together to meet the needs of their students.

Many preschool and elementary educators are aware of and want to try new approaches but have questions like these: How can I make these great ideas work in my classroom? How can I organize instruction to enable young children to carry out their own science investigations and engineering design projects? What are the children in my classroom capable of? What kinds of instruction lead to meaningful learning? How can I engage each one of my students?

What's the purpose of this guide?

This guide is intended to help answer these and other questions. Through longer, detailed examples—called cases—and shorter examples, it shows what high-quality teaching and learning in science and engineering can look like for preschool and elementary school children. Through analyses of these examples and summaries of research findings, the guide points out the key elements of a coherent, research-grounded approach to teaching and learning in science and engineering.

The goal is to inspire practitioners at the preschool and elementary levels to try new strategies for science and engineering education, whatever their level of experience.

What is the research base for this guide?

This guide is based primarily on a 2022 report of the National Academies called *Science and Engineering in Preschool through Elementary Grades: The Brilliance of Children and the Strengths of Educators.*[2] To produce that report, a committee assembled by the National Academies reviewed and synthesized research on effective science and engineering instruction for children in preschool through grade 5.

---

[2] National Academies of Sciences, Engineering, and Medicine. (2022). *Science and engineering in preschool through elementary grades: The brilliance of children and the strengths of educators.* The National Academies Press. https://doi.org/10.17226/26215

The *Brilliance and Strengths* report covers fundamental insights about children's learning and describes how to design, implement, and support instruction and curricula that bring out the inherent brilliance of every child. It discusses the implications of this research for classroom practice at the preschool and elementary levels. The report emphasizes that children as young as age four can "do" science and engineering as a pathway to learning the core ideas and concepts of these fields. To make this happen, instruction should build on children's natural curiosity, ideas, interests, and experiences in the world around them. It should engage them in investigating phenomena and designing solutions, as scientists and engineers do.

This practitioners' guide is intended to bring to life the findings of the *Brilliance and Strengths* report and to present practical issues touched on in that report from a teacher's perspective. This guide also draws from other sources, including articles and books suggested by the National Academies' committee members and staff; interviews with educators and researchers; conferences, webinars, and other events organized as follow-ups to the study; published curricula; and websites of research organizations and educator associations.

The instructional strategies described in this guide are supported by evidence presented in the *Brilliance and Strengths* report. For that report, the National Academies reviewed many types of research studies on preschool and elementary science and engineering. The members of the study committee applied standards of evidence to determine whether to include specific strategies in their report. They carefully considered the strength of the evidence and other factors. In some cases where the evidence for a strategy was sparse but the strategy addressed an important area of focus or filled a gap, the committee decided to include the strategy but noted the quality of the evidence in their report. The *Brilliance and Strengths* report also looked at evidence that indicated which strategies were most appropriate for various grade bands (preschool, K–2, and 3–5).

What are the sources of the cases and examples?

The cases and examples in this guide illustrate real experiences from classrooms and other learning environments, although in some instances, revealing details have been changed. These examples come from studies of classroom practice and research-based curricula reviewed by *Brilliance and Strengths* committee members, as well as from the other sources described above. Cases are labeled with the heading "Ready, Set, Investigate!" or "Get Set, Design." Each of these extended cases is followed by an "inspiration board" where key insights from the case are discussed.

All of the teachers, administrators, students, and parents cited in this guide are referred to by pseudonyms. Education researchers, however, are referred to by their real names and affiliations.

These cases and examples are meant to spotlight particular aspects of preschool and elementary level practice that other educators can learn from. They are not meant to be "perfect" illustrations of instruction, but, rather, to portray how educators in real environments are implementing a new vision of instruction in which children explore the natural world and solve problems much as scientists and engineers do. In addition, each case is a snapshot from a broader sequence of lessons and units; many aspects of that bigger picture have been omitted. As you read and think about these examples, please be respectful of the educators who have bravely opened their thinking, practices, and classrooms to researchers, curriculum developers, and colleagues so that other educators can learn.

Who can use this guide?

Practitioners who work with children in preschool through grade 5 or who support teachers at this level can find useful information in the pages that follow. This audience includes teachers, instructional coaches, principals, and other administrators. Curriculum developers, teacher educators, and others involved in science and engineering education may also find helpful ideas in this guide.

How is the guide organized?

Chapter 1 gives a broad picture of the possibilities and promise of new approaches to teaching science and engineering in preschool through grade 5. It introduces the principles that underlie these approaches and the key elements of effective instruction. The chapter also emphasizes the benefits of these approaches for children and the assets that preschool and elementary educators bring to this work.

Chapter 2 illustrates the competencies that even very young children have for learning science and engineering. It shows how learning is a dynamic cultural and social process that occurs in many different contexts. The chapter also discusses ways to bring out the proficiencies of all children by infusing attention to equity and justice into your instruction and creating a caring classroom community.

Chapter 3 explains the fundamentals of instruction anchored in investigating scientific phenomena and designing solutions to engineering problems. It introduces "sensemaking"—the active process children use to figure out how the natural and designed worlds work and to solve problems. It goes on to describe features of meaningful science phenomena and engineering design problems for learning.

Chapter 4 explores how you can deepen students' sensemaking. The chapter discusses key aspects of sensemaking, including strategies to guide children as they plan investigations and design tasks, analyze and interpret data, develop and use models, construct explanations, and argue from evidence.

Chapter 5 looks at the critical role of children's talk and other forms of discourse in helping teachers elicit and refine students' ideas and advance their sensemaking. It begins with strategies for creating a positive environment so that children feel comfortable, safe, and willing to interact and learn with their peers.

Chapter 6 discusses approaches to assessments that are compatible with instruction anchored in investigation and design.

Chapter 7 describes how instruction in science and engineering can be intentionally integrated with teaching of other content areas, such as language arts and mathematics, in ways that reinforce learning, make efficient use of classroom time, and maintain the integrity of targeted learning goals.

Have a go!

The strategies and examples in the guide are offered to inspire you as a teacher, leader, or other education professional involved in science and engineering education. They are intended to show some possibilities and build confidence about taking steps in these directions, rather than to lay out models to be implemented in their entirety all at once.

So dip into the chapters that follow. Use this guide to prompt different ways of thinking about your students and your practice. Start by implementing something that intrigues and excites you. Within the broad elements of these new approaches, you can then adapt to your own strengths and those of your students.

Share this guide with colleagues. Discuss it at team meetings. Try out something you may have been hesitant to do, secure in the knowledge that others have also tried and successfully gone down this path. Above all, trust that the assets that have brought you this far as an educator will carry you into new territory.

Moving to
"I Can Teach Like This"

If you teach science to children in preschool through fifth grade, or if you lead or support teachers, then you know that exciting changes are underway in science and engineering education. Perhaps your state's science standards call on students to use the practices employed by scientists and engineers to build their knowledge of the crosscutting concepts and core ideas of science and engineering—an approach called "three-dimensional learning" (defined below). Perhaps your district or school is implementing a curriculum in which students ask questions, investigate real science phenomena or engineering problems, and leverage their growing knowledge to explain a phenomenon or design a solution.

This new approach weaves together all three dimensions of learning as laid out in the National Academies' 2012 *Framework for K–12 Science Education: Practices, Crosscutting Concepts, and Core Ideas*[1]—scientific and engineering practices, crosscutting concepts, and disciplinary core ideas. When engaging in three-dimensional learning, students:

- Use **practices** (dimension 1) similar to those used by scientists and engineers.

- Learn and apply **crosscutting concepts** (dimension 2) of science and engineering.

- Develop and deepen their understanding of the **disciplinary core ideas** (dimension 3) of specific science disciplines and engineering.

Examples of how this looks in a classroom are given below.

This new approach is powerful, but it can be quite different from what many preschool and elementary educators are used to doing. Maybe you're moving in the right direction but are unsure how to get there. If so, you're in good company. Many

---

[1] National Research Council. (2012). *A framework for K–12 science education: Practices, crosscutting concepts, and core ideas.* The National Academies Press. https://doi.org/10.17226/13165

preschool and elementary teachers feel invigorated by the possibilities of what they and their children can do with new approaches to science and engineering, but they have questions and a bit of apprehension about how to do it well.

What does this new approach to science instruction look like?

Consider the example of Ms. Ochoa, a fourth-grade teacher who teaches all subjects. She understands the value of science instruction in which students conduct their own investigations. But last year, her students weren't as motivated about their science activities as she would have liked, and she wasn't sure they really understood the disciplinary core ideas and crosscutting concepts she was teaching. For example, Ms. Ochoa taught students about the motion of waves by having them work at a water table where they created different-sized waves, floated small objects in the water, and

observed how the objects moved. Although the children enjoyed the hands-on activity, they couldn't really articulate what they were trying to figure out.

This year, Ms. Ochoa is using some lessons from science instructional materials suggested by a colleague that are aligned to the NGSS and compatible with three-dimensional learning. Ms. Ochoa likes that the materials provide her with a structure for implementing three-dimensional learning while empowering students to identify questions and problems that matter to them and to plan, conduct, and refine their own investigations. She has already been using open-ended questions and prompts to guide student discussion, but this new approach enables her to sharpen those skills, as illustrated in the following case. Please note that the activities highlighted in the case are segments of a longer unit, designed to extend over 12 class periods of about 45 minutes each.

The mystery of the mess on the beach[2]

It's Thursday afternoon—science time in Maya Ochoa's fourth-grade classroom. Ms. Ochoa is showing the children slides of a beach littered with thousands of bags of tortilla chips and a large, damaged shipping container lying on the sand nearby. (The photos are from a real event in which a tractor-trailer-sized container washed up on the shore of Hatteras Island, although the children don't know that yet.) "What do you notice?" Ms. Ochoa asks, "What do you wonder? What caused this to happen?"

The goal of this unit is to help students understand how waves move and how this affects floating objects. To pique students' interest in these ideas, the lesson centers on the question, "Why do some things wash up on the beach and others don't?"

Students volunteer several responses of things they noticed or wondered about after viewing the slides, such as these:

- People at the beach are picking up bags.

- The container had a hole and was on the beach.

- Did people litter on the beach?

- Did the container fall off the ship?

Ms. Ochoa doesn't render judgments about right or wrong answers. The purpose is two-fold: to get students brainstorming about how the chips got on the beach, as well as to surface students' current understanding about how waves affect various floating objects. If she listens closely enough, she can use student ideas to frame subsequent investigations. A variety of ideas emerge, such as a truck crashing on the beach or a container falling out of a ship at sea. Ms. Ochoa gently presses for more details, as in this example:

Ms. Ochoa: So, I hear you saying maybe there was a cargo ship. Maybe there was a truck. Maybe this container was carrying [chips] and it fell off, fell out, had some kind of accident. Jorge, tell us more.

Jorge: I just had a theory that the truck went into like a boat, like one of those boats that bring in cars and stuff . . . I was thinking it might have been like the Titanic, like it hit something . . . and then the crate was opened when the ship sank. And the [chips] bags had air in it so it probably went up and then a tidal wave probably or a tsunami picked it up, swooshed on the beach . . .

After reading a news article about the actual event at Hatteras, students refine their ideas, but they continue to be puzzled about how something as large as a shipping container could wash up on shore. Ms. Ochoa prompts them to draw models of their initial ideas, which include the container being pushed by the wind, moved by waves, or pulled by sea animals. Note she is not looking for a right answer, but is instead using these initial models as a way to support students in sharing their thinking.

In the second class session, students take further charge of their learning by identifying various questions they want to investigate, such as these:

---

[2] This case is based on McGill, T. A. W, Housman, G., & Reiser, B. J. (2021). Motivating three-dimensional learning from students' questions. *Science & Children, 59*(1), 54–60; and McGill, T. A. W., & Novak, M. (2019). NextGen Science Storylines, grade 4 waves and ocean structures storyline, https://www.nextgenstorylines.org/why-do-some-things-wash-up-on-the-beach-and-others-dont

- How can something heavy like the container float on water for days without sinking?

- How does water push heavy stuff?

- How does water form into waves?

To narrow down the possibilities, the students share their questions with the class and group similar questions into categories using a "question board" provided by the teacher. Next, the students come up with suggestions for the kinds of investigations they could do in class to help answer their questions. To guide students toward something concrete without telling them what to do, Ms. Ochoa again uses purposeful questions, as in this example:

Ms. Ochoa: What could we investigate to answer the rest of our questions? Samantha, what do you want to do?

Samantha: I think we should solve what makes the waves, because maybe that will give us "Why did the [chips] get all the way to the beach?"

Ms. Ochoa: Anybody else want to add on?

David: We could get a bucket of water, and put in something that floats, and see if waves can push it.

In the third lesson of the unit, students make waves in a bucket, but they realize the bucket is too opaque for them to really see what they're doing. They refine the process by using a transparent water bin and a paddle to make waves. After some experimentation, they figure out how to make taller or shorter waves and to vary the space between waves. On another day, the students take the next step by adding floating objects to the wave bin to represent the chips. Their efforts don't turn out as

they expected. Regardless of what kind of waves they make, they can't push the floating objects to the opposite end of the bin, which represents the shore.

Ms. Ochoa resists the temptation to tell them what to do to get to the "right" answer. Instead, she proposes that maybe the wave tank is not a close enough stand-in for the ocean. She suggests that the class look at a website showing cargo ships at sea in real time. After noticing that these ships tend to travel close to the Atlantic Coast shore, and after studying maps of the ocean floor in that area, the students realize that the depth of the ocean water gets shallower closer to land. The class revises their investigation of how floating objects interact with waves, but this time they slant the wave tank by propping up one end to replicate a slanted ocean floor. And it works! The objects at the deeper end move to the shore. The class creates a final consensus model to explain how the chips got to the beach (see Figure 1-1).

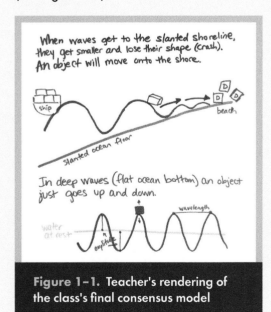

Figure 1-1. Teacher's rendering of the class's final consensus model

Source: McGill et al., 2021.

Inspiration board: Learning from the case

The preceding case illustrates how new approaches to science and engineering instruction can make learning exciting and effective.

- **The instruction weaves together all three dimensions of learning.** In Ms. Ochoa's unit on wave motion and floating objects, the students engaged in the three dimensions of learning:

  - **Practices** (dimension 1): In this case, for example, students *planned and conducted an investigation* and developed models to explain how a floating object washed onto the beach.

  - **Crosscutting concepts** (dimension 2): Students applied the crosscutting concept of identifying *patterns* to help account for why floating objects repeatedly moved to the shallower end of their slanted wave tank. This led them to develop an explanation of how wave action can move a large floating container across the slanted sea floor to the shore.

  - **Disciplinary core ideas** (dimension 3): One learning goal of Ms. Ochoa's unit was the disciplinary core idea that when *waves move across* the surface of deep water, the water goes up and down in place; there is no net motion in the direction of the wave except when the water meets a beach.

- **This is not just hands-on instruction—it's minds-on.** This type of instruction is far removed from a cookbook-type experiment in which children follow a step-by-step recipe to observe, for example, which of four nails will rust when treated with different substances or left untreated. In the preceding case, Ms. Ochoa encourages students to think by asking them open-ended questions and putting them in charge of planning the investigation. They wonder, question, explore, revisit assumptions, and apply what they are learning to solve a problem. Because students arrive at their findings by investigating, gathering evidence, and revising their understanding, the disciplinary core ideas and crosscutting concepts that they learn are more likely to stick with them.

- **Children investigate a meaningful phenomenon.** A meaningful phenomenon for science learning is a circumstance or event that is interesting, puzzling, and connects to children's experiences outside of school. The phenomenon of thousands of bags of a common brand of tortilla chips strewn across a beach next to a shipping container sparks students' curiosity. It's something that really happened and has implications for the environment. "The teacher told me to do it" is not a great motivator. When children follow their own curiosity, or get inspired by the curiosity of their peers, they are more motivated to investigate, stay engaged, and learn. Phenomena that are relevant to children's lives outside of school in their homes and communities can be particularly powerful.

- **Children's discussions and interactions with each other are avenues for learning.** The unit in this case includes several opportunities for children to work together, negotiate, and make decisions as a group. This approach to instruction recognizes that learning is a social process, not just an individual one. As children collaborate, they are exposed to new ideas and different perspectives and build knowledge together. They are also mirroring the collaborative practices used by scientists and engineers.

- **The teacher's role differs from that of traditional instruction but is just as critical.** In a classroom like Ms. Ochoa's, the teacher guides children as they frame and investigate their own questions, instead of simply explaining to students how to do something and giving them facts and answers. As part of this new role, the teacher plans carefully, with the help of good instructional materials, and structures a caring, collaborative environment in which students can learn. As the students ask questions, consider phenomena, and plan investigations, the teacher pays close attention, as Ms. Ochoa did, to students' ideas to determine what they need to support their individual and group learning. The teacher observes and asks questions that guide students toward understanding and solutions. The teacher also listens intently for science ideas in the everyday vocabulary of students. As students investigate, the teacher monitors their progress, carefully checking for understanding and providing consistent, clear feedback, as Ms. Ochoa did.

You may need time to become comfortable with and adept at these new strategies and role. But just as Ms. Ochoa learned from and improved on how she had taught in previous years, you, too, can build on things you already do as a teacher.

Why is three-dimensional learning effective?

The three-dimensional approach better reflects what scientists do than traditional instruction does. In three-dimensional learning, students are continually expanding and deepening their knowledge, rather than memorizing a collection of static science facts. The three-dimensional approach is also more rigorous—and vigorous!—than

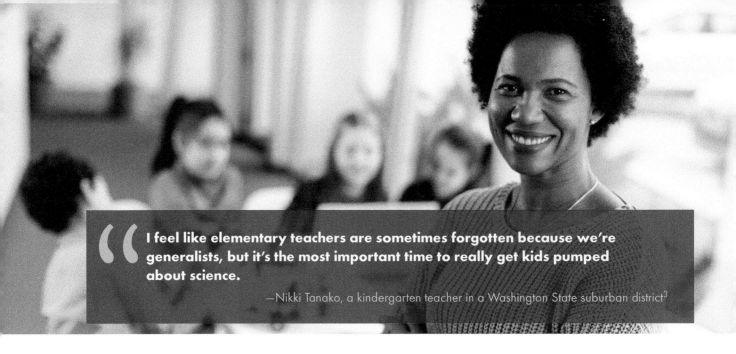

"I feel like elementary teachers are sometimes forgotten because we're generalists, but it's the most important time to really get kids pumped about science.

—Nikki Tanako, a kindergarten teacher in a Washington State suburban district[3]

traditional instruction because it recognizes that students need to do more than just learn the content (core ideas) of science disciplines; students also need to understand the crosscutting concepts that connect disciplines and be able to actively *use* their growing knowledge to answer questions and solve problems, as real scientists and engineers do. So, a three-dimensional approach shifts the goal of learning from "defining and understanding" science ideas to "developing and using" knowledge.

Is three-dimensional learning appropriate for younger children?

The answer is *absolutely*, as evidenced by the main source for this guide, the National Academies' *Brilliance and Strengths* report.[4] Three-dimensional learning leverages children's intense curiosity about the world around them and their eagerness to investigate. Children as young as preschool age can think and act like scientists and engineers as a pathway to learning the concepts and core ideas of these fields.

What kinds of instruction make three-dimensional learning happen?

Research synthesized in the National Academies' *Science and Engineering in Preschool through Elementary Grades: The Brilliance of Children and the Strengths of Educators* report has identified certain key features of instruction that help preschool and elementary teachers engage children in three-dimensional learning.

Box 1-1 summarizes these and other key features of effective science and engineering instruction.

---

[3]National Academies of Sciences, Engineering, and Medicine. (2022, March 16). *Taking stock of science standards implementation: A summit—supporting 3D instructional shifts coffee talk* [Webinar]. https://www.nationalacademies.org/event/03-16-2022/taking-stock-of-science-standards-implementation-a-summit-supporting-3d-instructional-shifts-coffee-talk

[4] National Academies of Sciences, Engineering, and Medicine. (2022). *Science and engineering in preschool through elementary grades: The brilliance of children and the strengths of educators* The National Academies Press. https://doi.org/10.17226/26215

BOX 1-1

KEY FEATURES OF INSTRUCTION FOR 3D LEARNING

- Leverages children's existing ideas, interests, and curiosity about the world

- Anchors instruction in investigating phenomena and solving design challenges

- Engages children in science and engineering practices as a means to build knowledge and use that knowledge to answer questions and solve problems

- Allows children to take the lead by asking their own questions, making sense of and recording what they observe, planning and conducting their own investigations, and testing and refining their explanations and solutions

- Focuses on learning experiences that are meaningful and relevant to real-world issues and to children's family, community, cultural, and other contexts

- Embeds attention to equity and justice throughout instruction rather than tacking it on.

As a central feature, effective science instruction is anchored in *investigations* of meaningful phenomena—observable circumstances, events, or processes in the natural or built world. High-quality engineering instruction is anchored in *designs* of objects, systems, or processes to solve a problem or meet a need.

This type of instruction may look different from how you've taught in the past. Or, you may have tried some of these strategies and are ready to continue refining your practice in this pedagogy. Implementing these approaches requires teachers to learn, plan, and practice. But take heart. You may already be doing some of this, and you can start with small steps, as discussed later in this chapter. Implementing instruction for three-dimensional learning is an ongoing, long-term process.

Moreover, there are *many* different ways to teach that are aligned to the *Framework for K–12 Science Education* and centered on investigation and design. The later chapters of this guide provide details to help you with that process.

What does instruction anchored in science investigation and engineering design look like?

To see the key features of three-dimensional teaching and learning in action, let's look at a case from a K–2 curriculum designed to integrate science, engineering, and literacy development.[5] The units are centered on a puzzling phenomenon. Each lesson is organized around five components: students *ask* questions, *explore* a phenomenon or problem, *read* (or are read aloud to), *write*, and *synthesize* what they have learned. Most of the lessons are 60 minutes and the components allow the teachers to break up a lesson to spread it across multiple days.

This case spotlights portions of a unit for kindergarteners called the Boxcar Challenge. In the unit, students investigate how soapbox derby cars move in different ways without engines. They also take on an engineering design challenge by building small model boxcars out of cardstock and determining how to make their cars move farther, move faster, and turn around an obstacle. Learning experiences such as these, chosen with specific outcomes in mind, help students understand different aspects of motion and the forces of push and pull.

The case is just a snapshot—the Boxcar Challenge unit consists of 10 lessons of carefully designed and sequenced activities.[6] Box 1-2 shows the student activities for each lesson of the unit.

As you review the case below, notice how Ms. Bassi, the teacher, taps into young children's curiosity by inviting them to wonder aloud and ask their own questions. Throughout the unit, she also uses her own questions to elicit children's thinking and get them to clarify and build on their own and others' ideas. She attends to their non-verbal gestures as well.

Note, too, how children of kindergarten age can do investigations and engineering design. They propose ideas about how to change the motion of the boxcars. Using the model boxcars they construct, children investigate and gather evidence about how different types of pushes and pulls affect the boxcars. Finally, they design and test various solutions to make a boxcar move faster and farther and turn around an obstacle.

Another remarkable aspect of this case is how the instruction integrates opportunities for children to develop their language skills and literacy while engaging in science and engineering. Through reading, writing, and drawing activities, children

---

[5] SOLID Start (Science, Oral Language, and Literacy Development from the Start of School), a K–2 curriculum developed by Michigan State University professors Tanya Wright, who specializes in language and literacy, and Amelia Gotwals, who specializes in science education.

[6] The full curriculum materials can be accessed at https://education.msu.edu/research/projects/solid-start/curriculum/

record their ideas and observations, develop models, and advance their understanding of how the boxcars move.

BOX 1-2

SUMMARY OF LESSONS IN THE BOXCAR CHALLENGE UNIT

How can we make things move fast, far, and turn?

Lesson 1. Students explore toys and record observations about how they move. They also ask questions about how toys move.

Lesson 2. A text is used to introduce the idea of force. Students build on their exploration with toys in Lesson 1 to explore whether they can use a push or a pull to cause toys to start moving.

Lesson 3. Students are introduced to the boxcar derby challenge through a video and to the engineering design cycle through a book. They brainstorm ideas to make a boxcar move faster, farther, and turn based on what they learned about pushes and pulls in Lesson 2.

Lesson 4. To connect to the boxcar derby phenomenon in Lesson 3, students are introduced to models in engineering. They build and explore a model boxcar.

Lesson 5. Drawing on what they have learned about how to make toys move, students investigate how the strength of a push affects speed and distance.

Lesson 6. Students expand on what they learned about push forces to investigate how the height of a ramp affects speed and distance.

Lesson 7. To continue learning how to make boxcars move faster and farther, students investigate how weight affects boxcar movement. They consider the force required to start their boxcar moving and how far their boxcar travels with different weights.

Lesson 8. Students conduct an investigation to determine what happens when their boxcar collides with a block.

Lesson 9. Based on their previous investigations, students develop engineering design plans for how to make their boxcars move fast and far and turn through an obstacle course.

Lesson 10. Students construct and test their design solutions to make their boxcars move fast, far, and turn.

Source: Edwards, K. D., Gotwals, A. W., & Wright, T. S. (2020). The Boxcar Challenge unit: Integrating engineering design, science, and literacy for kindergarten. *Science and Children, 57*(5). https://www.nsta.org/science-and-children/science-and-children-january-2020/boxcar-challenge-unit

GET SET, DESIGN!

Kindergartners progress faster and farther by investigating and designing[7]

In a kindergarten class in a rural Midwestern district, Gia Bassi, a veteran teacher, begins lesson 3 of the Boxcar Challenge unit by showing her students a short video. In the video, children participating in a soapbox derby try to make their boxcars move fast and talk about their experiences. The students in Ms. Bassi's class watch with interest.

Noticing, wondering, brainstorming

When the video is done, Ms. Bassi asks her students two questions: "What did you notice happening with the boxcars?" and "What do you wonder about the boxcars?"

The room fills with whispers as the children formulate their responses and rehearse them by talking into their cupped hands. Then, the children turn and talk to a partner about their ideas. After a few minutes, Ms. Bassi, using a list of names that she checks off to encourage fair participation, calls on students to share something that they or their partner had noticed or wondered about. She records their responses so all students can see them, as in these examples:

Elena: I noticed some of them went a little bit faster.

Daniel: I noticed it had a pedal to push to make them go faster.

Sierra: I wonder where the steering wheel is that makes it move.

Lyle: I wonder if the things float like a boat because they kind of look like a boat if you take off the wheels.[8]

In a whole-group discussion. Ms. Bassi poses additional open-ended questions to encourage the children to clarify their ideas. "How do you think the boxcar started moving?" she asks. Looking at Trent, she asks, "What do you think?" Trent responds with words and gestures:

Trent: I think, I think they get the momentum to move. (Trent stands and sways from side to side.) I think they like push that pedal down. So they can move (shows pushing with right hand). You see that wooden thing (shows hand raising)? It goes down (drops hand) when they push that thing (kicks leg out toward an imaginary pedal).

Ms. Bassi: OK, and then what happens after?

Trent: They . . . they start moving.

Ms. Bassi: The boxcar? The boxcar starts moving?

[7] This case is based on West, J. M., Wright, T. S., & Gotwals, A. W. (2021). Supporting scientific discussions: Moving kindergartners' conversations forward. *Reading Teacher, 74*(6), 703–712; Edwards, K., Gotwals, A., & Wright, T. (2020). The Boxcar Challenge Unit: Integrating engineering design, science, and literacy for kindergarten. *Science and Children, 57*(5); interviews with Amelia Gotwals, Tanya Wright, Jeanane Charara, and two anonymous teachers using SOLID Start for instruction; and SOLID Start curriculum materials: https://education.msu.edu/research/projects/solid-start/curriculum/. The case uses a single pseudonym to represent two different teachers cited anonymously in West et al., 2021, and in Edwards et al., 2020.

[8] West et al., 2021, p. 707, Figure 1.

Trent: It's like a push (shows both hands pushing forward).

Ms. Bassi: I see.

After this discussion, Ms. Bassi reads aloud a book to the children about how engineers solve problems. She then continues this same lesson by asking children to work with a partner and brainstorm ideas for making model boxcars move fast, far, and around an obstacle. The children record their ideas through writing and drawing, while Ms. Bassi circulates and strikes up conversation to draw out each child's thinking.

Once the partners have had a chance to brainstorm, Ms. Bassi brings all the children together again and asks them to share their ideas, which she records on a chart (Figure 1-2). To scaffold students in giving feedback on their classmates' ideas, Ms. Bassi gives them this sentence frame: *I agree (or disagree) with _____'s idea because _____.* During the course of a longer discussion, students use this sentence frame to comment on one peer's suggestion of starting the boxcar from a higher ramp to make it go faster:

> **Gavin:** I agree with their idea because higher means going faster, like a sled.
>
> **Jordan:** I disagree with them because our group said you should push the car more times.
>
> **Ms. Bassi:** Could both of those solutions work?
>
> **Jordan:** No, ours is going to be make it go faster. (A lot of talking)
>
> **Ms. Bassi:** Okay, okay, well we don't know yet, right? We are going to investigate these ideas.

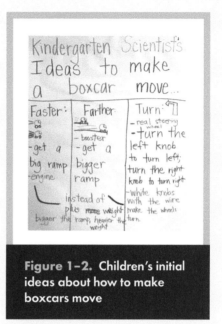

Figure 1–2. Children's initial ideas about how to make boxcars move

Source: West et al., 2021.

The design challenge

Across the last seven lessons of the unit, children build their boxcars and explore how to make them move by pushing and pulling. They stage boxcar collisions and observe the effects. After multiple investigations, they design solutions for making their boxcar travel by using a ramp, pushing harder, adding washers for weight, and other ideas. Throughout these seven lessons, they add to and refine their ideas, make claims, and provide evidence to support their claims.

As children work individually and in small groups, Ms. Bassi asks questions to get them talking, encourage their participation, and help them clarify their ideas. While she's careful not to discourage students whose responses are incomplete or technically incorrect, she uses astute questions to guide them to a clearer explanation. For example,

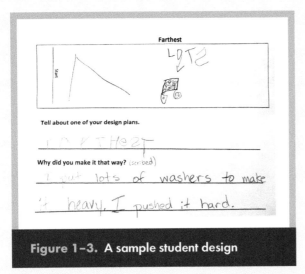

Tell about one of your design plans.

_____

Why did you make it that way? (scribed)

I put lots of washers to make
it heavy. I pushed it hard.

Figure 1–3. A sample student design

Source: Edwards et al., 2020.

after children move boxcars on ramps and predict how far they will go with high or low ramps, they write or draw their observations and ideas, working independently or with partners. (Figure 1-3 shows an example of a child's drawing.) During this phase, Ms. Bassi walks around the room and asks each child what they're thinking and what they're writing or drawing. She follows up with questions that nudge each child to clarify or fill in missing information (e.g., *What makes you think that? Were you surprised by what happened? I see your drawing; how will you make your car turn? What else could you try?*)

When Marcus and Destiny suggest using a longer ramp to make the boxcar go farther, Ms. Bassi initiates a conversation (abridged) with this question:

Ms. Bassi: So why do you think a bigger ramp might make it move faster? . . . What's going to happen? What do you think?

Marcus: It . . . it (moves his right hand in an upward slope over his head quickly, stops abruptly when Destiny talks over him).

Destiny: Well, the smaller ramp, it's gonna get . . . it's gonna go like this. Where it landed (motions on her paper to show where the car starts on the ramp and then where it stops).

Ms. Bassi: (Nodding and making eye contact with Destiny and looking at her paper as she explains.)

Destiny: But then a bigger ramp (positions her finger on a box on her sheet representing the top of the ramp) would make it go bigger (moves her finger like a pretend car to show the car going farther across the paper from the start of the ramp) and faster because it is a bigger ramp (again moves her finger like a pretend car from the top of the ramp and down the page) than before.

Marcus: And then it would go like right here (puts his finger on his sheet at the top of the ramp and moves it all the way off the page to the edge of the table, tapping it repeatedly where the car would end its motion).[9]

---

[9] West et al., 2021, p. 709.

Notice the important role of non-verbal gestures in the above exchanges. Also, notice how throughout the unit, Ms. Bassi introduces vocabulary carefully and purposefully. She encourages and supports students in using key vocabulary from read-alouds as they investigate and construct explanations. She does not "pre-teach" or front load vocabulary instruction. For example, after the children experiment with pushing the model boxcars with their hands, Ms. Bassi initiates this conversation:[10]

Ms. Bassi: What else do we know from our investigation?

Bao: The boxcar moved slower when I pushed with my finger . . .

Ms. Bassi: What did we learn from our book? What is a push a type of?

Multiple students: A force!

Ms. Bassi: Okay, so who can tell me what we learned about forces today?

Ava: The hand was a big force and the finger was small.

Theo: The hand force was big and made the boxcar go faster.

A critical part of every lesson is to synthesize the results of the investigations. Students reflect on and share their design solutions with the class. They consider such questions as what worked well about their designs, what didn't work, what evidence supports their conclusions, and what they could improve. As a group, they summarize claims that can be made based on their investigations (e.g., *boxcars with the tallest ramp went the farthest*) and what evidence they used to figure that out. They think about which steps of the engineering process, such as testing models, helped them answer the key question from the beginning of the lesson. They determine which questions they have answered and what questions remain.

Children in various types of districts have responded well to the instructional strategies in the Boxcar Challenge, says Virginia Stott, a kindergarten teacher in a Midwestern district that encompasses suburban and rural areas:

I think the curriculum offers kids that opportunity to really think about science and look at it in an interesting way. It's not drudgery for them; they love it. They look forward to it. They ask, "Is science on the schedule today?"[11]

---

[10] This conversation is abridged from the original version in Edwards et al., 2020, and uses different teacher and student pseudonyms.

[11] Interview, Feb. 4, 2022.

Inspiration board: Learning from the case

The preceding case illustrates how a teacher might implement portions of various lessons anchored in investigation and design. The case highlights several key aspects of instruction that you might find informative or inspiring.

- **Young children can do, enjoy, and learn from scientific investigations and engineering design tasks.** The Boxcar Challenge case demonstrates how instruction centered on an engineering problem can motivate young learners. Children in the case not only designed and improved solutions to the boxcar challenge, but also recorded data and generated and refined explanations for why objects move in certain ways. It helped that the initial problem was framed in a specific and engaging way around soapbox derby cars, rather than as a general invitation to consider in the abstract how objects move. The children acted on and continued to develop their love of making things, discovering new ideas, and solving problems, while deepening their understanding of core ideas in physical sciences, such as force and motion.

- **Students have more control over their own learning than in traditional instruction.** The things students noticed and wondered about after seeing the video of moving boxcars set the stage for the questions to be explored. The initial questions about how to make a boxcar move fast, move far, and turn were open-ended, rather than presuming a "right" answer. This open-ended aspect allowed students to grapple with key science ideas in action and in tandem, rather than memorizing the effects of various forces abstractly or in isolation. Students shaped what and how they investigated by coming up with initial explanations. They refined and deepened their understanding by modeling, discussing alternatives, testing various approaches, and other activities.

- **Instruction values all children's contributions.** In the Boxcar Challenge case, the teacher used strategies to give all students opportunities to contribute to discussions. All children also participated in the investigations and design challenges. Students were encouraged to share their ideas through talk and gestures and through writing and drawings. Their ideas were recorded in visible ways and discussed in small and large groups. Students had various options for communicating their understanding (e.g., drawing, speaking, gesturing, modeling, and labeling, in addition to writing), which is particularly helpful to multilingual learners.

Everyone's contributions were publicized and valued. These aspects can help children develop a positive identity as knowledge generators and doers of science and engineering.

- **Teachers scaffold and support students' learning through questions and other means.** Giving students greater control over key aspects of learning doesn't mean that teachers cede responsibility. As the case shows, Ms. Bassi subtly guided the progress of students' learning by asking them well-considered questions. She sought clarification, introduced vocabulary at key points, and reminded students of what they read or did in previous lessons, among other strategies. She did this for the whole group and for individual students. In the exchange with Trent, for example, Ms. Bassi prompted Trent to clarify his responses and be a bit more specific. She listened to his words and watched his gestures to gauge his understanding. This can be a form of assessing what students know and how they are understanding the phenomenon.

- **A well-designed curriculum can support teachers in changing instruction.** The broader curriculum that contains the Boxcar Challenge includes detailed lesson plans, assessment guidance, links to NGSS performance expectations, and several other resources for each unit. In general, a well-designed curriculum can support you with many aspects of instruction. It can provide a structure and coherent flow for your lessons and classroom activities. It can help you identify meaningful phenomena and anticipate children's questions. Many curricula include teaching tips and examples of student responses, along with ideas for formative and summative assessment and other valuable materials.

- **Language arts and literacy can be integrated smoothly into science and engineering education.** This case shows how science and engineering instruction can be designed to incorporate many opportunities to help early elementary children develop literacy. These include reading and listening to read-alouds, writing explanations, and drawing models. When well-designed, this type of integration can be particularly beneficial for multilingual learners.

On a related note, you can teach children science vocabulary like *force* and *motion* not as "words on a wall," but by first getting them to explore the concepts and practices represented by the vocabulary words. After students incorporate academic terms into their everyday language, these newly-learned academic words can then go on a word wall. This process helps students develop fluency with new vocabulary as they continue to grow their conceptual understanding through investigation.

Chapters 3 through 7 of this guide describe these and other practices in depth, using additional cases and examples.

How does this approach to instruction benefit preschool and elementary children?

Many arguments for elevating science education in elementary school focus on preparing children for the future. For decades, scientists, educators, political leaders, and others have emphasized that it's critical to start science instruction in the elementary grades to prepare students to take more challenging courses later and eventually to find good STEM-related jobs. Advocates for early science education also point out that society as a whole benefits from scientifically literate citizens who can make informed decisions about issues related to topics such as health and the environment.

Science and engineering learning for children's "now"

The above points about preparing children for their adult futures are valid. There are also other, equally compelling reasons why children need high-quality science and engineering education that focus on children's immediate experiences.

From an early age, children deserve to experience the wonders of science and the satisfaction of engineering for their *present* selves. Instruction anchored in investigation and design is conceived to stoke children's enthusiasm for science and engineering and nurture joy. It gives children the means to answer their own questions and solve problems that grab their interest.

These approaches hold more promise for engaging all children in science and maintaining a lifelong interest in the field than traditional instruction does, with its focus on amassing knowledge of science facts. The new approaches honor how students learn and retain information by building a robust conceptual understanding.

Positive identification with science and engineering

When children investigate phenomena and engage in design challenges, they begin to see themselves as people who know and can do science and engineering. This attitude will serve them well throughout their lives, whether or not they pursue careers in these fields. Adults, as well as children, who know and identify positively with science have the confidence to make personal decisions using science, can critically

evaluate scientific information in the media, and can make informed decisions as community members.

Enhanced opportunities for engineering education

Opportunities for children to participate in engineering design are rare in preschool and elementary classrooms. This is much to the detriment of young children, because engineering education enhances their learning in several ways. Instruction centered on design problems can engage children's curiosity much like informal play. It can strengthen children's problem-solving and critical thinking and give them practice in fine motor skills and social skills. Creating something physical can help children make connections between the human-designed world and the core ideas and cross-cutting concepts of science and engineering.

Equity and justice

Instruction anchored in investigation and design can advance equity and justice for all students. This type of instruction starts from the premise that all children, especially those from historically marginalized groups, can engage in scientific and engineering practices when they are supported and can learn and use core ideas and crosscutting concepts from these disciplines. This support takes many forms, such as connecting with children's own interests and culture, recognizing their ideas and contributions

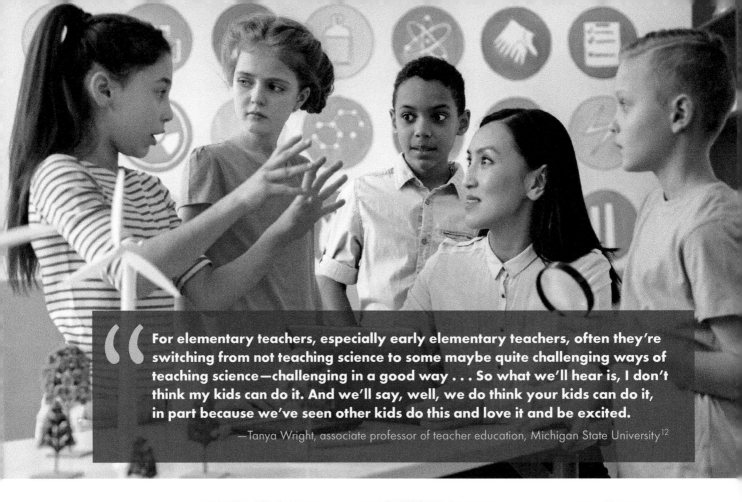

> **For elementary teachers, especially early elementary teachers, often they're switching from not teaching science to some maybe quite challenging ways of teaching science—challenging in a good way . . . So what we'll hear is, I don't think my kids can do it. And we'll say, well, we do think your kids can do it, in part because we've seen other kids do this and love it and be excited.**
>
> —Tanya Wright, associate professor of teacher education, Michigan State University[12]

as valid, providing multiple ways of demonstrating proficiency, and being thoughtful about teacher-student and student-student interactions. In Chapter 2 and subsequent chapters of this guide, you'll find further discussion of ways to embed equity and address issues of justice throughout your science and engineering instruction. This can range from enhancing children's opportunities and access in science and engineering to increasing representation and identity in science and engineering, and from expanding "what counts" as science and engineering to seeing science and engineering as a part of justice movements in your community.

How can I move toward teaching for three-dimensional learning?

Given the challenges, you may wonder, can I become effective and comfortable with instruction anchored in investigation and design? Can my students learn this way? The answers are yes and yes.

The purpose of this guide is not to intimidate you or add to your already heavy load, but to rejuvenate and inspire you, while building on your expertise and experience. In the chapters that follow, you'll find further examples of practitioners at the preschool and elementary levels who have taken small and larger steps to transform

---

[12] Interview, Dec. 10, 2021.

science and engineering instruction in ways supported by research. These educators work in different contexts and have varying levels of experience. Some have always loved science and were excited about trying new approaches, while others were more tentative. Some leaped all the way in, while others dipped a toe. Some started out alone and later found like-minded colleagues and mentors, while others entered as part of a professional development cohort. All of these practitioners have learned and grown alongside their students.

Rely on your strengths

Preschool and elementary teachers typically teach multiple subjects and may not have a specific background or expertise in science and engineering. As a result, you may feel somewhat overwhelmed by the vision of learning described in this chapter. Rest assured, however, that as a result of your breadth of experience, you bring many assets that can help you teach science and engineering subjects well. Among these assets are:

- An understanding of how children think and learn;

- An inclination to care for children and advocate for their well-being;

- Expertise in teaching reading and writing;

- A recognition of opportunities to connect across subjects;

- Repertoires for organizing small group work and whole class discussions;

- A capacity for building relationships with children and families;

- Inquisitiveness about the world and willingness to learn;

- Knowledge of a variety of teaching strategies;

- Experience with differentiating instruction for a variety of learners;

- Flexibility and resilience; and

- Other strengths that come from your own character and experiences.

Taking stock of your assets can give you the confidence to implement new approaches. And in building on your assets, you'll find an entry point that works for you.

Recognize that both early-career and more experienced educators can make changes

Teachers of all experience levels have successfully implemented instruction anchored in investigation and design.

If you're near the beginning of your teaching career, you may worry that you don't have as much science experience or as many tried-and-true strategies as experienced teachers. But you may have a fresh outlook, a strong desire to try something promising with your students, and an open and creative mind.

Perhaps you can relate to the situation faced by Christopher Pritchard,[13] when he was hired halfway through the school year by a Maryland school district. "We were still using the old curriculum, which was out of packets," he said. And this old curriculum "wasn't actually consistent with how we wanted to be teaching science." The next year his school adopted a new curriculum. "Really, it was diving right in, because that's all we had. And I didn't have the experience of having the old lessons be something that I wanted to fall back on, to try and teach a lesson that I thought was really good from the packet days."

That lack of experience worked in his favor. Mr. Pritchard and his principal took a course on the NGSS, where he met the district science specialists and was invited to join the district's science cohort. "I dove in feet first," he reported. "And it kind of just felt right—of all the curriculum that we teach, the science curriculum is the one that I think is most consistent across the board and feels put together and complete."

Another new teacher from an urban New Jersey district, Lily Hamerstrom,[14] had a similar experience when she was hired mid-year to teach fifth-grade science and mathematics. "I was just thrown into it," she said. "And to be honest, science was on the back burner. I was a new teacher, and math was really what the district cared about at that point. And I didn't have a background in science."

With her district in the midst of implementing the NGSS, Hamerstrom was expected to teach an active-learning science curriculum adopted by the district. With limited opportunities for professional learning, she "winged it" by reading books and asking colleagues who taught all subjects. Eventually, her district became part of a pilot for a phenomenon-based curriculum developed at a university. After three years of professional development and support from the detailed curriculum and from other teachers and leaders, Hamerstrom was implementing phenomenon-based instruction with growing competence and confidence. She offers this advice to other new

---

[13] Group interview, Jan. 12, 2022.
[14] Interview, Mar. 7, 2021.

teachers: "The NGSS can be overwhelming if you look at it as a whole . . . But once you break it down, you can see it's really nothing to be scared of . . . So, just dive into it."[15]

If you're a veteran teacher, you may face a different set of circumstances. You may have a reliable set of teaching strategies and lessons that you've polished over time and that have produced satisfactory results. You may be comfortable leading instruction and skilled at managing your classroom. These experiences may make you a bit wary about shifting more control to students.

Veteran teachers may recognize some commonalities in the experience of Barbara Germain,[16] from Maryland. "It did take some time for me to realize that I'm not the one to just tell them what is happening—that it really should be more inquiry-based and more discovery-based," she said. Her district's approach encourages students to identify the questions to pursue. She responded in this way:

> [W]e tried to lead [the students] in a certain direction. But ultimately, the students then get to plan their investigations. And that took me a while to really latch onto, because it's hard to think, like, oh, they're not going to get to this idea . . . I've learned over the years that they do get there, you know, in some way or another. And I think that is probably the biggest piece of growth that I've had as a teacher . . . giving students control.

To sum it up, whether you're an early-career or veteran teacher, you have assets and tools that will help you implement new approaches to science and engineering education.

Start small and give it time

For a variety of reasons, you may not be able to implement a whole new approach all at once. The examples and advice in this guide can provide a starting point.

Teachers, researchers, and professional development providers offer these suggestions for easing into new approaches to instruction that integrate knowledge and practices of science and engineering:

· Use the structure and supports that come with your curriculum if it's aligned to the three dimensions in the National Academies' *Framework for K–12 Science Education.*

---

[15] Interview, Mar. 7, 2022.
[16] Group interview, Jan. 12, 2022.

- Focus on those strategies that you find inspiring, exciting, or promising and that draw on what you already know and can do. And then expand from there.

- Start with a lesson, activity, or strategy that you feel most comfortable with to build confidence and expertise, then move toward strategies that may have initially seemed intimidating.

- Take to heart this advice from Delia Harewood, a fifth-grade teacher in an urban district in the Northeastern U.S.: "If something didn't work out really well, that is an opportunity to learn."[17]

As you gain in confidence and experience, you will develop a broader repertoire of strategies that work for your classroom.

Remember that implementing instruction anchored in investigations and design problems is a long-term process of continual improvement. Recognize that it gets easier and better over time. Any curriculum that is aligned with the National Academies' *Framework for K–12 Science Education* "is going to be rigorous and difficult in a good way, in an exciting way, but it's not going to happen overnight," said Alison Haas, project manager for the Science And Integrated Learning (SAIL) research lab at New York University. Teachers need time to learn a new approach and "play with it in their classrooms," she explained.[18]

Adapt and differentiate

Within the broad elements of instruction anchored in investigation and design, not everyone will teach the same way. Even the best-designed approaches need to be adapted to your own context and your own students. Instructional strategies, content, activities, and types of support will vary by grade levels, based on the developmental level of the students. Implementation may also differ according to student strengths and needs, cultural and community contexts, geographic location, district policies, and more.

The chapters that follow provide guidance and examples for different grade levels, interests, and needs.

---

[17] Interview, Jan. 3, 2022.
[18] Interview, Mar. 7, 2022.

Seek out support to help overcome challenges

As you implement new or revised approaches, you'll face the inevitable challenges. You can overcome some of these challenges yourself or with support from colleagues. Other systemic and policy challenges may require actions on a larger scale.

Many educators have already confronted and dealt with the same challenges you're likely to face. Support can come from a variety of formal and informal sources—your teaching colleagues, your school or district instructional coaches and leaders, professional development providers, curriculum providers, local colleges and universities, and virtual communities, as well as science museums and other informal science learning environments. The epilogue to this guide talks about how educators can help each other move down the path toward three-dimensional instruction and get over the bumps.

Don't be put off by systemic and policy challenges

Not all challenges can be addressed at the classroom level; some may be outside your immediate sphere of influence. In these situations, you can do as much as you can by thinking creatively and working collaboratively, but at some point, you'll need to depend on leaders to address larger structural or policy issues.

One big systemic challenge in preschools and elementary schools is finding time to teach science and engineering well. In self-contained classrooms, just a small slice of the K–5 school day—about 20 minutes daily, on average—is typically devoted to science instruction.[19] You want your students to pursue investigations and engineering design challenges, but you need a larger chunk of time. This situation is exacerbated by the pressure teachers at these levels face to meet testing and accountability requirements in English language arts (ELA) and mathematics. You would like to make time for high-quality science instruction, so what do you do?

Carefully and purposefully integrating instruction in science and engineering with ELA or math can help with the time crunch. Some teachers using the curriculum described in the Boxcar Challenge case have made time for a 60-minute science lesson by teaching science and social studies on alternate days, dividing longer investigation and design activities across two days, and shifting time from their reading/language arts block to teach aspects of a science or engineering unit that incorporate reading, writing, and language development. You can learn more about integrating across content areas in Chapter 7. That chapter emphasizes the importance of maintaining a focus on meaningful science instruction while supporting development of students' proficiency in ELA and mathematics.

Enlightened principals and other leaders have made it a priority to organize school schedules to allow for more time and consistent time for science and engineering instruction. If your school schedule does not reserve enough time or your principal has not shown flexibility on this issue, you can sometimes collaborate with other teachers to bring up this issue with school leaders.

Teachers are also dealing with a host of broader workforce challenges. Teachers are expected to do more than ever and to persevere under pressure from a variety of sources, even as staff shortages have become more widespread. Because of this, many teachers and education leaders feel stressed and fatigued, and that must be acknowledged. Educators are generally resilient and have demonstrated their commitment and adaptability time and again. For this guide, the key question is how you can draw

---

[19] Banilower, E. R., Smith, P. S., Malzahn, K. A., Plumley, C. L., Gordon, E. M., & Hayes, M. L. (2018). *Report of the 2018 NSSME+*. Horizon Research, Inc. https://horizon-research.com/NSSME/2018-nssme/research-products/reports/technical-report

on the capacity you have to teach science and engineering in the most effective ways to help children learn.

You can do this!

Moving toward this type of teaching and learning can be intimidating—and rewarding. The learning curve may be steep at first. Not every lesson will be a triumph, but that's part of the process of teaching. Fifth-grade teacher Delia Harewood summed it up in this way:

> There has been so much trial and error with how to adapt to the instruction. And I've had to get over my fear of failure, so to speak . . . But once you are comfortable, you have confidence. And because you're confident now, you may feel like, 'I can do better. I can now learn something that I may not know that much about and get support along the way.'[20]

---

[20] Interview, Jan. 3, 2022.

Bringing Out the Brilliance of *All* Children

I named a lot of bugs, and different kinds of animals and things . . . I said, "How are all those things alike?" and [a student who had been struggling in school] raised his hand and said, "They're all things in a food chain." And so, Mrs. X and I were like, Wow! He has received a lot of academic support this year, but he always, I mean, he's been just like a little science sponge. He can tell you every single thing, all the time, every day, he's the first one to answer, and that's really cool. I'm always saying to him, "I can tell you are thinking and talking like a scientist."[1]

In your interactions with children, you've no doubt been amazed at times by how a child's mind works. Starting from infancy, children show curiosity about their surroundings. To make sense of their world, young children look, watch, and listen. They explore and ask countless questions: *Where do worms live? Why does ice float? Why is it cold in the winter?* They try something new, and then try it again to see if it turns out the same.

This intense curiosity and enthusiasm for learning are part of what the National Academies of Sciences, Engineering, and Medicine's 2022 *Science and Engineering in Preschool Through Elementary Grades: The Brilliance of Children and the Strengths of Educators* report calls the "brilliance of children."[2] Research has opened up a new perspective on what young children can do and how and where they learn science and engineering. Central to this perspective are four main ideas, discussed in this chapter:

- **Even very young children have competencies that facilitate learning in science and engineering.** By the time children start school, they bring many assets

---

[1] Wright, T. S., & Gotwals, A. W. (2017). Supporting kindergartners' science talk in the context of an integrated science and disciplinary literacy curriculum. *The Elementary School Journal, 117*(3), 513–537.

[2] National Academies of Sciences, Engineering, and Medicine. (2022). *Science and engineering in preschool through elementary grades: The brilliance of children and the strengths of educators.* The National Academies Press. https://doi.org/10.17226/26215

that will help them learn science and engineering, with the right support and scaffolding.

- **Children learn about science and engineering in a range of contexts in addition to school.** These include natural and human-made environments, as well as social, cultural, and community contexts. Variations in these contexts shape what and how children learn.

- **Learning is a social and cultural process.** Children learn by interacting with people, engaging with ideas and things created by collectives of people, and participating in social and cultural groups. A key part of this social process involves forming an identity as someone who knows and can do science.

- **By emphasizing the brilliance of all children, three-dimensional learning offers new ways of infusing equity and justice into science and engineering education.** When children begin at an early age to use science and engineering practices to solve problems, this opens up more ways for them to build knowledge and demonstrate competency. Three-dimensional learning is more flexible in what counts as science so that students can bring their ideas, reasoning strategies, ways of being, and ways of valuing into the classroom. Instruction centered on interesting, relevant phenomena and problems can cultivate the joy and wonder of science. It can also better motivate all learners by providing connections with issues of justice in their everyday lives.

By emphasizing children's competencies and social contexts, these ideas shake up some traditional assumptions about how children learn science and engineering. These ideas are also foundational to many of the instructional strategies described in this guide. If you understand what children bring to learning, you can design robust instruction that leverages their competencies and links with their social contexts.

What competencies do children have for learning science and engineering?

Children can do a lot. Even very young children observe the world around them and try to figure out how and why things work. They are natural investigators and can be persistent in their quest for understanding. They often approach problems in creative, playful, and intuitive ways. At times, they may say things that surprise you for their unique viewpoint or way of thinking about a problem.

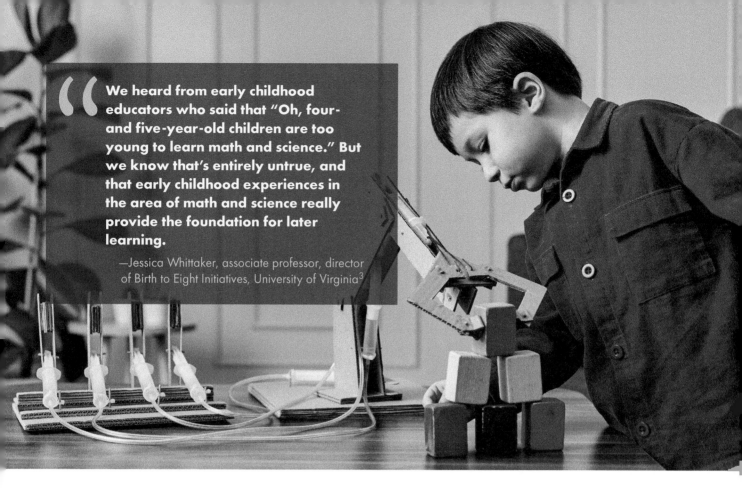

We heard from early childhood educators who said that "Oh, four- and five-year-old children are too young to learn math and science." But we know that's entirely untrue, and that early childhood experiences in the area of math and science really provide the foundation for later learning.

—Jessica Whittaker, associate professor, director of Birth to Eight Initiatives, University of Virginia[3]

Children of preschool and elementary age can think in ways that go beyond the immediate and concrete. They can connect ideas and think conceptually. They can generate explanations and communicate their reasoning. This example from a real preschool environment shows the competency of children:

Susan Emmanuel, a preschool teacher, has set out wooden blocks, ramps, and balls for her young learners to play with. Her real purpose is to encourage the children to engage in engineering design. Savannah and Dory have erected a ramp and are ready to test it. Dory carefully releases a wooden ball down the ramp. The students (and Ms. Emmanuel) watch closely as the ball slips off the side of the ramp and rolls away.

Dory: That did not work.

Ms. Emmanuel: Well, what can you do to make your ball stay on the ramp?

Dory: We need to block the side and build a wall to keep the ball on the ramp.

The two children construct a barrier that's "just high enough to protect the ramp, but not so high that it will topple over." They release the ball, which rolls

---

[3] Interview, Feb. 11, 2022.

straight down the ramp, through a tunnel, and across the finish line they have fashioned.

Savannah: Ah! That is better. We solved the problem![4]

As children grow older, they can communicate their reasoning and learn from others. They can collect and analyze data and can make remarkable models to represent their ideas. They can develop explanations of how or why something happens. They can consider actions based on their fairness and impact.

Virginia Stott,[5] a kindergarten teacher who uses the phenomenon-based curriculum described in Chapter 1, is impressed with the quality of her students' discussion after they have completed an investigation:

> They model it, and then we discuss what worked, why it worked, or why it didn't work. So, the investigations allow for very—I feel like for five-year-olds—very in-depth conversations.

Asset-based instruction

Children come to school with an inclination for investigation and many other assets that can help them learn and do science and engineering. To fully recognize and bring out the brilliance of children, you may need to change your perspective and teaching strategies to take an asset-based approach to instruction. Asset-based instruction involves listening to and observing children to determine what they bring to the table. Children's talk and actions reveal what they know and don't yet understand, how they are thinking about a problem, and what ideas they have that you can build on. This emphasis on listening for and noticing students' ideas is different from the traditional priorities of covering a lot of science content, making sure children do what's expected, and praising "right answers" only. The traditional approach doesn't leave much time to discern what children already know and can do, how they are thinking, and how you draw on their initial brilliance to help them learn and grow.

Teachers who take an asset-based perspective look for and honor a wide range of proficiencies in children, such as innovative problem solving, unique scientific observations, persistence through a task, and insightful inferences. They take note of and reward behaviors like expressions of curiosity, risk-taking, tolerance for ambiguity, and the use of strategies to improve focus. Not only can this help you to

---

[4] Gold, Z. S., Elicker, J., & Beaulieu, B. A. (2020). Learning engineering through block play. *Young Children,* 75(2), 24–29. The excerpt uses different teacher and student pseudonyms than the original article.

[5] Interview, Feb. 4, 2022.

expand what counts as science or engineering, but this also supports a more equitable classroom where all children can develop identities as people who do science and engineering.

A caring classroom culture

Creating a caring classroom environment is an essential part of asset-based instruction. In a caring classroom, every child is celebrated as a capable knower, doer, and communicator. Children feel safe sharing their ideas and taking risks. You can foster this type of environment through actions like these:

- Noticing and welcoming all children's contributions;

- Recognizing and valuing children's diverse experiences, ideas, ways of engaging, and means of expressing their understanding;

- Making children feel safe to participate fully in the classroom;

- Ensuring that children feel they belong to a community and see their work as important to others;

- Designing collaborative activities so that children learn with and from each other;

- Leveraging children's social, cultural, and linguistic resources as foundational for learning;

- Establishing classroom norms that emphasize respectful relationships among children and between children and the teacher; and

- Building relationships with children, families, and communities.

In a caring environment, children's social-emotional needs are met along with their academic needs. You can draw on children's emotional dimensions to support learning and understand that for some children, particularly those from marginalized communities, there are emotional risks in engaging in certain activities. For example, an engineering design task that requires students to "work through failure" can be risky for children who have received negative feedback or punishment for making mistakes.

Instruction that brings out the brilliance of children can be fun, even liberating, for both students and teachers, as illustrated by fifth-grade teacher Delia Harewood.[6] In her science classes, Ms. Harewood has developed a range of unique strategies to create a positive and nurturing environment, build relationships, and spotlight each child's strengths. For example, once a week on "Thankful Thursdays," each student randomly picks another child's name from a cup and writes a note to that child commending them for something positive they did academically. "They have to pay attention because they can get anybody in their classroom, and they have to write a positive comment," says Harewood.

Chapter 5 lays out additional strategies for establishing a collaborative classroom environment.

In sum, educators can bring out children's assets and leverage them to develop children's ideas, practices, and motivation to learn science and engineering. As a starting point, you might examine how your own assumptions about children's competencies shape your teaching and how you might change your instruction to take a more asset-based approach.

Where does learning happen?

Children learn about science and engineering in many different contexts before they enter school, and they continue to learn in multiple contexts outside of school. Anywhere can be a place for learning, anyone can facilitate learning, and any experience can be a learning occasion. Children are learning all the time, in both planned and serendipitous ways.

Children learn by interacting with nature and human-made systems. Contexts for learning can range from a neighborhood playground to a science museum with state-of-the art, interactive simulations; from a classroom to a forest; and from grandma's kitchen to a safe view of a construction site.

The family context

These contexts encompass more than physical places. Children learn by interacting with people, as discussed later in this chapter, so that contexts for learning include social and cultural groups. The learning that happens in these social and cultural group settings will tend to use the language(s) that are spoken by these communities. As children grow older, their contexts for learning become more numerous and complex and often overlap.

---

[6] Interview, Jan. 3, 2022.

The family—including parents, siblings, extended family, and others acting in parental roles—is the first context in which children start to learn. In addition to providing learning experiences at home, families connect children with other contexts for learning science and engineering, whether through examining cracks in the sidewalk to finding biodiverse ecosystems, discussing how food appears in the grocery store, or tracing where trash goes after it disappears from our homes.

Learning in nature for schools and families

Educators in preschool through grade 5 can improve instruction by helping students make connections across contexts and leveraging what each of these contexts has to offer. An example of this type of instruction comes from a project that takes science education outdoors for children in pre-kindergarten through grade 5. Developed by university faculty working with educators, families, and community partners, the project includes an instructional model and materials[7] that emphasize equity and learning relationships among schools, families, and cultural communities.

The instructional model is organized around coherent "storylines" consisting of units that build sequentially on one another. There are storylines for teachers to use at school and in outdoor natural settings and a companion set of storylines for families and children to use at home and in their own outdoor investigations. (The family materials are available in English, Spanish, and simplified Chinese.)

In both the school and family storylines, students notice and wonder about things they see on outdoor "wondering walks." After conducting their initial wondering, children identify "what should we do" questions about science issues that matter in their communities. These "should we" questions engage children in researching and deliberating about issues with ethical implications for the environment and society, such as *Should we remove invasive species from our parks?* These "should we" questions prompt the need for new knowledge, and classrooms develop investigations that will help them answer such queries using evidence. Students, with support from their teacher, develop and investigate questions and use scientific practices such as collecting data and creating models. The storylines also encourage children to make connections to their personal experiences, family and community knowledge, and cultural practices.

In the following case, pay attention to how Ms. Hopper, the teacher, uses students' questions and interests arising from outdoor investigations to connect science learning in school with family, social, and cultural contexts for learning.

---

[7] Available at http://learninginplaces.org/

Should we let the leaves be? Field-based learning[8]

Mona Hopper, a White teacher in a Spanish immersion classroom, leads her kindergarteners and their families on a series of science "wondering walks" near their school in the Fall. During these walks, children make direct observations of plants, animals, and other aspects of nature and generate "I wonder" questions. The children record their observations by writing or drawing. As part of these lessons, Ms. Hopper also invites families to take these kinds of walks in their neighborhoods using materials developed for families.

During the wondering walks, Ms. Hopper realizes that among the many things the children notice, several learners show particular interest in falling leaves. In a follow-up lesson, Ms. Hopper and the class summarizes their various wonderings about leaves from the walks:

- Chantel's group wonders why leaves fall.

- Gigi's group wonders why the school's landscaper clears the leaves off the school courtyard with a leaf blower and what he does with the leaves he removes.

- Nang's family wonders why some plots in the community garden were covered with a blanket of leaves.

Based on these and other comments, Ms. Hopper proposes that the class, along with their families, investigate the following question: *Should we remove leaves or keep them on the ground?*

As part of their efforts to investigate this question, the class interviews the school landscaper, who explains that he removes the leaves because they get slippery when it rains and they clog the storm drains. In another interview, a community gardener reports that she covers her plot with leaves to help keep the garden moist, feed the creatures who live in soil, and keep the soil healthy with nutrients from decomposing leaves.

The students take stock of what they have learned from the interviews and what questions they still have, as in these examples.

Diego: It seems like they said two different things. It's good and bad to clear leaves.

Polly: I wonder if the leaves really make the soil healthier.

Ms. Hopper gives the students a handout to take home that encourages families to discuss the kinds of questions that children and families can investigate in class and at home to help answer the "should we" question. The next day, the class reviews the responses from families, which include

[8] This case is based on Learning in Places Collaborative. (2020). Learning frameworks: Ethical deliberation and decision-making in socio-ecological systems framework, 5–7. Learning in Places. http://learninginplaces.org/wp-content/uploads/2020/08/framework_socioecological-decisionmaking.pdf; Viewlands Elementary School. (2020, May 1). Focused Walk Relationships [Video]. YouTube. https://www.youtube.com/watch?v=chll98pbQkU; and Learning in Places Collaborative. (2020). Family science learning: Family storyline example: One family's field-based science journey. Learning in Places. http://learninginplaces.org/wp-content/uploads/2021/03/Family-Storyline-Worked-Example_sm.pdf

a variety of fruitful questions for investigation and opportunities for learning. For example:

- Do leaves hurt the soil if they're on the ground for too long?

- Is it better to mix leaves in the soil or just leave them resting on top?

- Will too many leaves attract bugs, rats, and mice?

- Is there another good use for leaves if they are taken away?

In the weeks that follow, children and families gather evidence by doing book and internet research and conducting additional investigations. One ambitious family compares the number of creatures (snails, worms, and isopods like roly-polies) they find living in places with and without leaves and look for patterns. They also observe how the number of creatures changes throughout the season. This family determines that these three types of creatures are more prevalent in areas with more leaf litter. They do internet research to better understand what worms and isopods eat and what role they play in keeping soil healthy. Eventually they reach a shared decision to rake their leaves but to put them in one area of the yard.

Families that don't have the capacity for this level of activity or don't have a yard to rake can still support their children's learning by taking seasonal walks around their neighborhood or a local park, noticing relationships between creatures and leaves, and comparing areas with and without leaf litter, for example.

Inspiration board: Learning from the case

The preceding case illustrates several noteworthy points about connecting science education with other learning contexts.

- **Field-based learning can spark students' curiosity in a different way than classroom learning.** It also provides meaningful opportunities for children to apply scientific practices and take on meaningful science topics. Even young children, like the kindergartners in Ms. Hopper's class, are ready for this challenge—they can ask insightful questions and make thoughtful observations.

- **Situating investigations in the local community and real issues emphasizes the social and cultural dimensions of learning.** Ms. Hopper used field-based experiences not only to make science learning more meaningful, motivating, and relevant to children, but also to connect what they are learning to considerations of community environmental issues.

- **Educators can find many openings for involving families in children's investigations and giving credence to family and community knowledge.** Ms. Hopper seized on small opportunities to open the door for family involvement. She proposed that the class, along with their families, investigate the central question of whether to remove leaves. By providing a take-home handout, she encouraged families to discuss possible questions that could be investigated in class and at home that would build toward answering this central question. She followed up by having the class review the families' responses, which produced a variety of fruitful questions for investigation—including some that the teacher hadn't expected—and learning opportunities.

You might be wondering how you can employ this type of learning experience within the curricular materials supplied by your district. Ms. Hopper did not need to involve families in considering and discussing the central question, the investigation launch, and the initial investigation planning. She could have posed the central question to the students only and assigned the handout as homework to be done by students on their own. Instead, she turned the conventions of homework into a more expansive opportunity when she asked students to use the handout to discuss at home *what they were going to be talking about anyway* in class the next day. The discussion in class the next day didn't hinge on family involvement but was certainly enhanced by it.

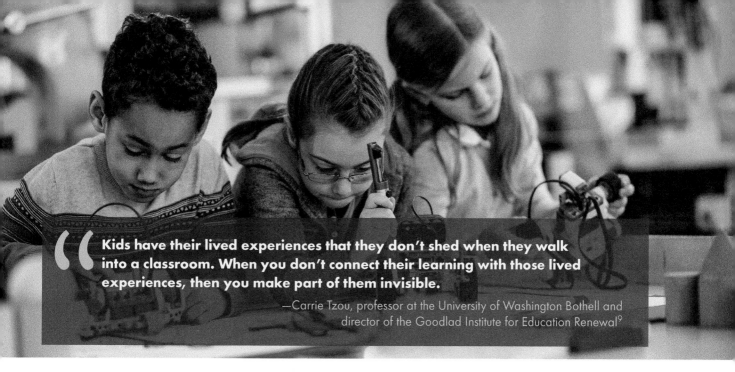

> **Kids have their lived experiences that they don't shed when they walk into a classroom. When you don't connect their learning with those lived experiences, then you make part of them invisible.**
>
> —Carrie Tzou, professor at the University of Washington Bothell and director of the Goodlad Institute for Education Renewal[9]

If no families had taken up the question, the class could have continued as planned, through small group discussions to develop an investigation idea.

Within the materials provided by your district, can you look for ways to invite families into the learning already happening in your classroom? Can you frame the central investigative question of your unit in a way that enables families to conceptualize it and generate ideas to support learning? Encouraging students to explore aspects of the unit in the context of their lives outside of school deepens their learning, boosts excitement, and allows students to test out their ideas before bringing them into class.

How awareness of multiple contexts can help with instruction

Different contexts offer different mixtures of situations, people, and resources to support learning. Children's experiences within these contexts not only build their knowledge and competencies, but also shape how they make sense of the world. What a child knows and can do is the sum of everything that child has experienced and learned across multiple contexts. From the child's perspective, it matters little where the ideas came from or in what order.

Why is it important for you as a teacher to pay attention to other contexts for learning?

·   **These contexts are a rich source of knowledge, experiences, languages, ideas, and practices that children bring with them to school.** By recognizing and

9 Anderson, J. (2020, December 3). What it means to learn science (No. 369) [Audio podcast episode]. In *Harvard EdCast*. Harvard Graduate School of Education. https://www.gse.harvard.edu/ideas/edcast/20/12/what-it-means-learn-science

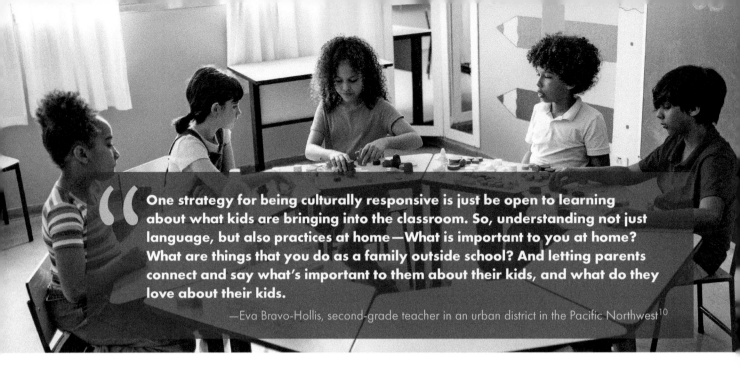

leveraging what children have learned and are learning in other contexts, you can improve classroom instruction.

- **The things children learn and do in other contexts may be different from what they experience in school.** This exposure to other contexts not only broadens and multiplies where and what children can learn but can also enrich classroom learning. For example, a diversity of experiences from other contexts can expose peers to new ideas and make for more stimulating science discussions.

- **When you appreciate, honor, and connect with families and other social contexts, you can better relate to children and understand how they learn.** This opens up more ways for you to reach children from all backgrounds and more partners to work with.

- **You can take advantage of other learning environments to expand on what children learn in school.** This might be done through a partnership with an informal learning environment, a field trip, an invitation for an expert to come to your class, or more casual means, such as making children and parents aware of a community site, like an urban garden.

How is learning a social and cultural process?

Children learn primarily from and with other people. They learn by interacting with teachers, classmates, caregivers, family members, friends, and countless other social contacts. In many ways, the social nature of learning corresponds with the collab-

---

[10] Interview, Jan. 20, 2022.

orative nature of science and engineering. Even when children learn from books and other educational materials, this is a social process because students are interacting with ideas, tools, and resources that have been developed by collectives of people.

Children's learning is also shaped by the practices, behaviors, and beliefs of the cultural groups they belong to and participate in. Cultural groups may influence how children observe, explore, relate to others, and come to understand things. That doesn't mean culture is static—cultural practices evolve in response to social, political, and geographic change.

For children from historically marginalized backgrounds, assumptions based on culture have often meant negative stereotyping and silencing. Because students learn when they explain in ways that make sense to them, effective instruction uses the asset-based frame discussed earlier. This benefits individual learners by affirming the value of their cultural ways of knowing and expressing ideas, recognizing their contributions, and reinforcing their identity as doers of science. Everyone in the classroom also benefits from having access to a broad range of experiences, diverse ideas, and resources for learning.

At the same time, viewing learning as a cultural process doesn't imply that you should make quick and easy assumptions about learners based on the one or more cultural groups to which they belong. Children participate in multiple cultural groups, and none of these groups is homogenous. It is possible to incorporate culturally derived ways of learning into instruction while also acknowledging that children vary in how they approach and absorb these cultural group experiences.

The following example describes how Native American families participating in a science education program in an urban forest preserve use Indigenous ways of knowing to help children learn about the natural world and their place in it.

Example

"Reading" the Tracks of a Deer[11]

Walking, reading, and storying land is a methodology that has long been embedded in Indigenous ways of building knowledge of the natural world. This methodology has multiple

---

[11] Based on Marin, A. (2019). Seeing together: The ecological knowledge of Indigenous families in Chicago urban forest walks. In I. M. García-Sánchez & M. F. Orellana (Eds.), *Language and cultural practices in communities and schools* (pp. 41–58). Routledge; and Marin, A., & Bang, M. (2018). "Look it, this is how you know:" Family forest walks as a context for knowledge-building about the natural world. *Cognition and Instruction, 36*(2), 89–118. https://doi.org/10.1080/07370008.2018.1429443

practices that are grounded in relational frameworks that **center** the agency of non-human organisms. The practices involve coordinating attention and observations in order to formulate stories or explanations specific to certain ecosystems or landscapes. As part of these practices, walkers attend to and observe elements of their surroundings, generate explanations, and find evidence.

Winnie Picotte, a mother, and Jonas, her six-year-old son, regularly participated in Urban Explorers, a field-based science program at an urban Indigenous community center. As a part of this program they routinely went on forest walks. They also went on forest walks as a family. On one of several family forest walks, Winnie and Jonas collaboratively read the land and developed "micro-stories" to explain what they were observing. Several minutes into the walk, Jonas encountered what he suspected was a deer trail. At Jonas's suggestion, they followed the deer trail. Excerpts from their recorded conversation illustrate how Jonas narrated a micro-story to make sense of their joint observations:

> **Jonas:** . . . there's a deer trail right here
>
> **Winnie:** That's a deer trail? . . . But how do you know?
>
> **Jonas:** Because . . . because I know what [a fellow Urban Explorer] does retracing the steps of a deer trail . . . they make trails by walking.
>
> **Winnie:** Oh.
>
> **Jonas:** . . . The deer musta crossed here . . . but then they got stuck . . . This musta been, like a long time ago when it's flooded, because lookit, there's a deer trail in the river.
>
> **Winnie:** Heh, heh, ya think those are deer trails in there?
>
> **Jonas:** Yah.
>
> **Winnie:** I think it just might be, like, holes. Holes in the riverbed.

Jonas was eager to find a place to cross the river, but Winnie was unsure. Eventually she followed. As they walked, Jonas assumed the perspective of a deer as he tried to figure out which way to go. Finally they reached a new path and again looked for deer tracks.

Winnie: . . . Look at these ones.

Jonas: Oh, those are deer . . . [taking a picture of the tracks]

Winnie: How come we didn't notice this going down there?

(Winnie suggests that maybe they had gone a different way, but Jonas proposes that what they are seeing are fresh tracks.)

Winnie: Because ya know how can you tell? How?

Jonas: Yeah, they're fresh because the dirt's still wet.

Through their moment-by-moment interactions, Winnie and Jonas built knowledge collaboratively. As they sought to interpret what they saw, they remembered important places they had seen on previous walks and compared the past (when a particular area was flooded) with the present. They used body movements, questions, and micro-stories to make their thinking visible and coordinate their observations. At times they imagined how other living beings may have behaved and the actions they may have taken as they developed explanations. They didn't always agree but they listened to each other's alternative explanations. The six-year-old Jonas made astute observations, such as the comment about the wet dirt.

The activities of walking, observing, gesturing, questioning, creating micro-stories, and thinking across time and space are more powerful in combination. They represent additional and important approaches for bringing science to life, connecting with culture, and making meaning. While these practices have roots in Indigenous ways of knowing, they are not limited to Indigenous communities, and could be adapted for classroom and field-based learning.

Instructional implications of the social and cultural nature of learning

These findings about learning as a social and cultural process show why it's important to organize your classroom to create opportunities for students to interact with and learn from each other. All of us learn by conversing and working with other people, and classroom peers are no exception. When students discuss and work together in small or large groups, they become aware of different ideas, learn from each other, and jointly construct knowledge. The creation of a positive, caring learning environment is one step toward acknowledging the social dimensions of learning and encouraging collaborative and supportive relationships among students.

Instruction that considers the cultural dimensions of learning can be enriching for all children. It signals to individual children that you value their experiences and gives them relevant ways to contribute and learn. It also invites a vibrant mix of ideas that energizes discussion, challenges ways of thinking, and encourages the growth of knowledge for everyone in the class. In your science and engineering instruction, you can leverage social and cultural resources by learning more about the cultures and family knowledge of your students and involving families in demonstrating and sharing their knowledge and practices.

We all bring our own perceptions of learning—and often our implicit biases—into this work. To effectively leverage student assets, take some time to reflect on how you communicate and assign competence to students and their ideas.

The critical role of identity in learning

Children are continually trying to figure out who they are and how they fit into different social contexts. This process, which contributes to identity formation, plays a central role in children's learning. Like learning, it is shaped by children's social and cultural environments. How and what children learn is related to how they see themselves and who they want to become. Learning is enhanced when children see themselves as people who can learn, know, and do science and engineering.

Children's identities in relationship to science and engineering are influenced by their social and cultural contexts. They are also shaped by children's previous opportunities to engage in science and engineering practices, their experiences in school, and other factors.

You may have heard a child say, "I'm not good at science"—the same child who yesterday watered a class plant "to help it get bigger." Even some children who do well in science in school say they "don't like it" or aren't interested in "becoming a scientist." They may not see themselves as "science people." These children may not yet know what constitutes science and engineering or may be influenced by damaging stereotypes about who does science. They may not understand how science and engineering are infused in their everyday lives and are not just the domains of people in STEM careers working in labs.

Children may need various kinds of support and reinforcement to begin to recognize themselves as learners, knowers, and doers of science and engineering. You can nurture this recognition by providing instruction that appreciates student's ideas and allows them to explore questions that matter to them. This type of instruction signals that being good at science consists of much more than knowing facts and scientific terms. As part of this process, you might examine your own sense of identity

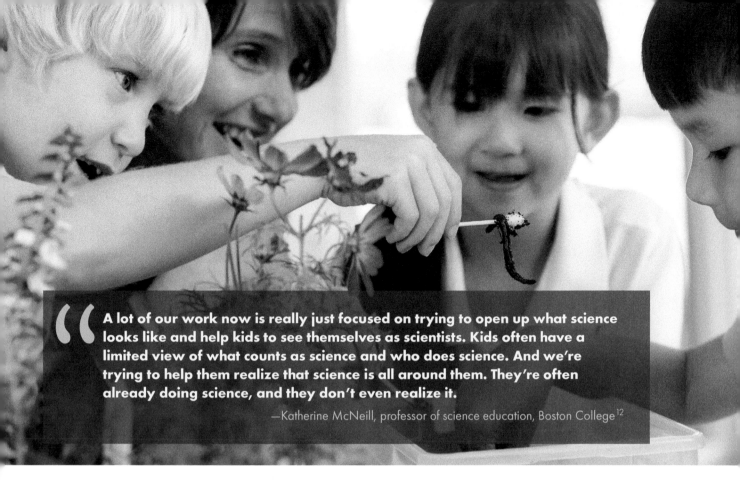

> A lot of our work now is really just focused on trying to open up what science looks like and help kids to see themselves as scientists. Kids often have a limited view of what counts as science and who does science. And we're trying to help them realize that science is all around them. They're often already doing science, and they don't even realize it.
>
> —Katherine McNeill, professor of science education, Boston College[12]

in relation to science and engineering—*Do I see myself as competent in these disciplines? Have I sought to develop a positive identity as a teacher and learner in these subjects?*—and how it has affected your teaching.

You can also provide sensitive support by recognizing and reinforcing a wider range of scientific behaviors. For example, when a curious child on a nature walk kicks at the dirt to better expose a colorful rock and shouts excitedly about their discovery, this is a mode of investigating. If a teacher interprets this behavior as disruptive and chastises the child, it can squelch the child's further engagement. But if the teacher commends the child for their explorations and observations and channels his enthusiasm into a meaningful discussion, then the child may see themselves as a budding scientist.

How can a commitment to equity and justice bring out the brilliance of all children?

While instruction anchored in investigation and design holds promise for bringing out the brilliance of all children, it doesn't automatically advance equity. Teachers must still be proactive and mindful to counteract damaging views about social and

---

[12] Interview, Mar. 14, 2022.

academic status assigned by peers or society. These ideas can also be perpetuated through curriculum and professional development. As a teacher, you have an essential role in creating a safe intellectual space for every student to learn and develop in the classroom. Some groups of students have been historically marginalized in science and engineering, by race and ethnicity, language background, gender, disabilities, and learning differences. Rather than seeking to "fix" children's deficits, effective instruction appreciates and builds on the assets of children from these groups, their families, and their communities, while also recognizing and attending to their needs.

A commitment to equity is fundamentally about doing what's best for every child. As a preschool or elementary educator, you care about children. You recognize that all children, and society as a whole, are stronger when children grow up to be active thinkers and scientifically literate problem solvers.

There are so many things that can be done to advance equity that it can seem overwhelming. To help educators consider these issues in a more manageable way, the National Academies' *Brilliance and Strengths* report organized approaches for addressing equity and justice into four categories. These approaches are arranged along a spectrum from the basic actions of removing barriers to access to the more proactive work of redressing injustices. Approaches 1 and 2 focus more on equity, while approaches 3 and 4 move toward justice.

This doesn't mean, however, that you need to implement these approaches in any particular order or that actions under the fourth approach are always more difficult than those under the second, for example. You can do them in any order and any combination; when these approaches are used together, they have a synergistic effect.

The four approaches are listed below, with an example under each of an action that you could take to implement that approach. These examples can help you set up instruction in which attention to equity is intrinsic, rather than something bolted onto an existing lesson or learning objective.

1. **Increase opportunity and access to high-quality science and engineering learning and instruction.** Ensure access to high-quality science and engineering instruction, facilitated by well-prepared teachers, through instructional practices, classroom norms, instructional materials, and supplemental experiences.

   Example: You see science "achievement gaps" as "opportunity gaps." You draw on children's cultural and language resources to give them broader ways to access science learning.

2. **Emphasize increased achievement, representation, and identification with science and engineering.** Improve learners' achievement in school science and

engineering by generating interest and fostering connections to science and engineering disciplines. Attend to the affective aspects of learning, such as motivation and belonging, to support students as they explore their identities as learners and scientists in the classroom.

Example: You use materials that include representations of scientists and engineers, and of children doing science and engineering, that cover a broad range of racial/ethnic backgrounds and people with disabilities. You connect science and engineering instruction with children's interests and identities. You position all children as scientists and engineers working together to explain phenomena and design solutions.

3. **Expand what constitutes science and engineering.** Examine and reframe who does science and what counts as science so that students have access to a wide range of resources. Make the most of different ways of understanding the natural and designed world, not only to support more children's learning and aid in the formation of an identity as one who can do science and engineering, but also to bolster science and engineering as disciplines.

Example: You learn to recognize and respond to the rich ways in which children make sense of the world, even if they don't reflect fully formed science ideas. You become attuned to the various ways in which children express their understanding, even if they don't look and sound like the norms and language of science and engineering that you're accustomed to.

4. **See science and engineering as part of justice movements.** Position students as powerful change makers within their communities by examining the relationship between science, equity, and justice. Start by prioritizing social projects that address communities' needs and goals, and then find a way for students to engage in science and engineering practices to advance those projects.

Example: You have children investigate how communities of color experience disparate effects of environmental pollution. You encourage children to talk to family members about local community development decisions and how they affect the full range of people, animals, and plants in the community.

A real classroom unit from Michigan shows how issues of environmental justice related to the quality of water in a community can be a focus of science investigation and learning.

Example

Water Is Life[13]

In Maisie Bauer's fifth-grade class in a charter school in a large Midwestern city, many students knew of or came from families where their municipal water had been shut off because they were behind on paying their bills. The school was also within 100 miles of the city of Flint, MI, where the city's drinking water supply had been contaminated with lead and other potential hazards. "The kids at that point knew about what was going on in Flint, because it was national and world news," says Bauer. "And so we started talking about it."[14]

The materials at Ms. Bauer's school were structured around project-based learning. These classroom discussions about access to clean water led Ms. Bauer to launch a year-long unit in 2016 that connected these local events with the study of water in science and the role of city services in social studies. *How does water support life?* was a guiding question for the year.

As part of this project, students read a news article outlining the dangers of lead poisoning and the Flint water crisis. They discussed the issue of water shut-offs and how they were largely focused on the city's Black residents. (Ms. Bauer is White, and the majority of students in her class in 2016 were Black.) The students made posters to summarize their understanding of lead poisoning and the water crisis. Next, they studied the human body's need for water, the properties of water, local waterways, and water scarcity. They debated the question, *Is water a human right?* Students started to reason that if clean water sustains life, people who cannot afford water fees should not have to pay for water. Later in the year, students traveled to a nearby river and took water samples.

As a culminating activity, the students made a video on water in their community. "We divided the kids into groups, and they wrote the script. And we filmed sections of the video," said Bauer. One student played the mayor, others played people whose water was shut off, and others stood in for members of the municipal water authority, among other roles. "They had a lot of fun with it. And they learned a ton," noted Bauer.[15]

---

[13] This example is taken from Davis, N. R., & Schaeffer, J. (2019) Troubling troubled waters in elementary science education: Politics, ethics & Black children's conceptions of water [justice] in the era of Flint. *Cognition and Instruction*, 37(3), 367–389. https://doi.org/10.1080/07370008.2019.1624548

[14] Interview, Feb. 3, 2022.

[15] Interview, Feb. 3, 2022.

By the end of the year, students spoke increasingly about water as a collective human right. They shared their insights about the social, political, and racial dimensions of access to water and the harmful implications of treating clean water as a commodity. And they used the science data they had gathered and the models they had studied (water samples, the particulate nature of water and of mixtures) to communicate their understanding of issues of water justice and their desire for change.

The Water Is Life example shows how a serious community issue can be a springboard for students to investigate a problem, learn about the relevant core science ideas, and use their growing understanding to take actions related to human justice. Children had already expressed concern about local water shut-offs and water contamination in another community, and the teacher used their interest to motivate them to learn about the science of water and social studies issues of local decision making and citizens' ways to influence policy. Students participated in a variety of activities that incorporated different modes of learning and that built on their family and community knowledge. They came to see that science knowledge can influence human decisions and be a tool for justice.

If you'd like to try something similar to the approach described in the example but think it's not possible because you have to use a certain set of instructional materials, consider where those materials might provide openings for you to make the connections to community issues. While the example describes a focused year-long study arc in a project-based learning classroom—a scale that may not be easily available to you—you can look for ways that fit your prescribed curriculum to leverage science and engineering practices and knowledge as tools toward building a more just society. Read through your next unit and consider how you can repackage some of the lessons. Look for the learning outcomes, essential questions, and investigations presented in the unit. Could any of these activities be connected to or contextualized within a real-world problem or event?

Valuing all students and establishing classroom norms

At the core, many of the actions you can take as a teacher to advance equity are about seeing, listening to, and valuing what students have to offer. There's a power in the messages that you transmit to students, even unspoken ones. If children interpret a teacher's actions to mean that only certain ways of expressing ideas are acceptable or that they will be misjudged if they give a "wrong" answer, they may choose to disengage. They may also choose not to take risks that are necessary for developing creative explanations or solutions.

A study of elementary school students[16] asked three Black boys and three girls—two Black, one White—who were working in teams on an engineering design challenge to rate themselves in engineering on a scale of 1–10. The self-assessments of the Black students reflected how well they felt they maintained "appropriate behavior" during engineering class. The assignment did not enumerate what defined "appropriate behavior," but left it open to interpretation by the students, as in these examples:

> **Clarice:** [I rate myself as] ten, because I'm a good student. I'm a good listener, I follow instructions, and I do what I'm supposed to do. And that's it.

> **Kevin:** Seven to eight because sometimes I can be off task and sometimes I can— sometimes I have my moments, like paying attention for the whole class and doing good.

These findings suggest that some children may feel vulnerable if they take a risk in putting forward ideas, critiquing another student's ideas, or negotiating teamwork. You can mitigate these effects by establishing a classroom environment that actively invites children to share ideas, learn from mistakes, and express themselves in their own ways and words, and that values everyone's contributions.

Translating these findings about learning into instruction

The findings summarized in this chapter describe pedagogy that is based on a robust body of evidence of how children learn. They reveal what you can do as an educator to capitalize on what students already know and can do related to science and engineering. Instruction is more meaningful when it draws on children's assets.

Moreover, these findings remind us that science and engineering really are everywhere. Children learn these subjects in myriad contexts and through rich social and cultural processes. Many opportunities exist to bring that learning into your classroom and connect with the knowledge and experiences children gain in other contexts. In a similar vein, you can move students into different contexts outside the classroom to enhance learning. Advancing equity and justice is achievable and starts

---

16 Wright, C. G., Wendell, K. B., & Paugh, P. P. (2018). "Just put it together to make no commotion:" Re-imagining urban elementary students' participation in engineering design practices. *International Journal of Education in Mathematics, Science and Technology, 6*(3), 285–301. https://doi.org/10.18404/ijemst.428192. The excerpt uses different student pseudonyms than the original article.

with valuing each child's strengths, actively designing instruction that's attentive to children's differences, and creating new science learning environments that work toward minimizing injustices. The chapters that follow explain how you can accomplish these goals.

QUESTIONS FOR REFLECTION

- What assumptions do I make about what children can and cannot do in science and engineering based on their age, grade level, social or cultural backgrounds, or other characteristics? Where do these assumptions come from? How do these assumptions influence how I communicate with my students?

- How can I broaden my view of what constitutes science and engineering? How might students demonstrate scientific behaviors in divergent or nontraditional ways, and how can I recognize and nurture these actions?

- What assets do I recognize in my students, in any academic and/or social context? How might these assets be beneficial in science and engineering learning? How can I partner with families to improve learning in science and engineering?

- Have I done things inadvertently that could have silenced or marginalized some children? Am I hesitant to expose children to practices or ideas that I think may be too "advanced" for their developmental level? If so, why?

- What is my own perspective on equity and justice? Have I seen these objectives as something to add on to existing lessons? How can I think differently about integrating these objectives?

Starting Strong with Investigation and Design

Instruction anchored in science investigations and engineering design can make learning more lasting and meaningful. You've probably used some type of investigations in your own science teaching, and you may have engaged students in some form of design work. But what do these concepts mean in the context of three-dimensional learning? What do investigation and design look like in pre-school and elementary school learning environments? How can you structure investigations and design tasks to not only engage and motivate all students but guide them to understand and use disciplinary core ideas and key practices of science and engineering? And how can you craft classroom experiences that advance equity and justice?

This chapter explains how you can get off to a strong start in centering instruction on investigation and design, an idea that we will continue to develop in later chapters.

What do investigation and design look like?

As used in this guide and in the National Academies' education work, *investigation* is associated with science and *design* with engineering, although the processes have much in common.

Distinguishing between investigation and design

Investigation is a process used to understand the world and develop new knowledge. In instruction for three-dimensional learning, an effective science investigation starts with and is anchored in an engaging phenomenon—an observable circumstance, event, or process in the natural or human-made world that can be investigated and explained using scientific practices and ideas. Children's desire to make sense of the phenomenon drives the investigation.

Engineering design aims to develop or improve an object, system, or technique in order to solve a human problem or meet a need. This is accomplished by using practices employed by engineers and an understanding of science. In an instructional setting, effective engineering design is grounded in solving problems that children feel are important and interesting to them.

The role of scientific and engineering practices in investigation and design

As students undertake investigation and design work, they use the eight science and engineering practices laid out in the National Academies' *A Framework for K–12 Science Education: Practices, Crosscutting Concepts, and Core Ideas:*[1]

- Asking questions (for science) and defining problems (for engineering)

- Planning and carrying out investigations

- Developing and using models

- Analyzing and interpreting data

- Using mathematics and computational thinking

- Constructing explanations (for science) and designing solutions (for engineering)

- Engaging in argument from evidence

- Obtaining, evaluating, and communicating information

Note that **engineering design is distinct** from science investigation in its application of some of the practices listed above. Since engineering aims to find practical solutions to particular human problems and needs, identifying and defining the problem is key. Students must test and refine their designs in light of the needs and perspectives of end-users. They must also balance various tradeoffs and consider social, cultural, and environmental impacts of their designs.

The eight practices listed above, which constitute the first dimension of three-dimensional learning, seldom proceed in a strict, linear way. They may be done in varying order and any combination. In a particular investigation or design task, some practices may be used more than others. Most importantly, both investigation and engineering design are **iterative**, meaning that some of these practices are repeated

---

[1] National Research Council. (2012). *A framework for K–12 science education: Practices, crosscutting concepts, and core ideas.* The National Academies Press. https://doi.org/10.17226/13165

but modified based on what's been learned and that possible explanations or solutions are continually refined to reflect new data and information. This flexible approach to using science and engineering practices contrasts with some forms of traditional instruction that direct students to follow a precise, step-by-step "scientific method" in their investigations, based on a flawed interpretation of how real scientists work.

Students' use of practices will become more sophisticated over time depending on both experience and age. Each practice can look very different in a first-grade classroom than in a fifth-grade classroom. For example, when first graders use mathematics to analyze data, they may count totals and look for simple patterns, while fifth graders might measure, calculate, and graph changes in area or volume over time.

Effective instruction centered on investigation and design is also **purposeful.** Children engage in the practices listed above not only to experience the delights and satisfaction of working as scientists and engineers do, but also for a clear purpose— to construct new knowledge and be able to use their growing knowledge to answer questions and solve problems. Each investigation or design task will integrate cross-cutting concepts (dimension 2) and core science or engineering ideas (dimension 3).

Thus, instruction anchored in investigation and design entails much more than hands-on learning, which has become a sort of mantra for science education. To be fruitful, investigations and design tasks must **activate children's minds** as well as their hands.

In addition, both investigation and design are **social** endeavors. Much of the work, including the eight practices, is done collaboratively. Even work done individually builds on the contributions of others and in turn contributes to group knowledge.

What does meaningful investigation look like in preschool and elementary settings?

To introduce what an investigation of a phenomenon looks like in the classroom, let's consider the case of Kellen Kearney, a first-grade teacher. Ms. Kearney uses an actual, unexpected event to pique children's curiosity about a phenomenon. This leads to a series of investigations that grow out of children's questions and observations. Notice how the investigations are designed with students' input and carried out by students, but with astute questioning, guidance, and planning by the teacher.

Learning about sound in the "too loud" class[2]

Kellen Kearney's first-grade class is a thriving, boisterous place in which children are excited about learning and work together well—especially when doing science. The children are surprised, and a little upset, to learn that a neighboring class has complained that they are too loud and has asked them to "keep it down."

Ms. Kearney gathers the children in a circle on the carpet to talk about their reactions.

> **Chan:** Our class is not bad! Why do they think we are too loud?

> **Monty:** How can we be too noisy when the door is closed?

As she listens to the children's frustrations, ideas, and questions, Ms. Kearney sees an opportunity to address the complaints of the neighboring class while maintaining her own students' enthusiastic investigations. She realizes she can use the issue of noise as an entry point to teach about sound, which is part of the first-grade curriculum. Before embarking on these lessons, Ms. Kearney confers with her colleague next door. Together they agree that Ms. Kearney's class will do the noisier bits of the lesson while the neighboring class is at specials.

Investigation stations

The next day at her class's morning meeting, Ms. Kearney tells the children that she's been thinking about their concerns about being too loud. She asks them if they want to find out more about how sounds are made, how they travel, and how they can be reduced or stopped. The children agree wholeheartedly.

Later that day, Ms. Kearney launches their investigation by setting up carefully planned "sound stations," each consisting of a group of similar objects. One station has tuning forks, another has drums of different sizes and shapes, a third consists of musical instruments including a harmonica and a toy guitar, and a fourth has pots and pans. The children, who are accustomed to working in groups, assemble into teams and go to their assigned stations. Ms. Kearney gives them a prompt—make and change sounds using just the objects at your station—and they start exploring. She also asks them to make observations and record them as drawings and words in their science notebooks.

At the drum station, for example, children use their hands and sticks to strike the drum head with greater and lesser force. They notice that hitting the drum harder makes a louder sound. When the children hit different parts of the drum and drum head, they perceive that some parts vibrate more than others and that different parts make different sounds. Children excitedly press the drums to their arms and faces so they can feel the vibrations.

[2] Based on Zombal-Saul, C., Starr, M., & Renfrew, K. (2014, July 22). Teaching NGSS in K–5: Constructing explanation from evidence [Webinar]. National Science Teaching Association; Zombal-Saul, C., Starr, M., & Renfrew, K. (2014, July 29). Teaching NGSS in K–5: Making meaning through discourse [Webinar]. National Science Teaching Association; and Zembal-Saul, C., Starr, M., & Renfrew, K. (2014, August 5). Teaching NGSS in K–5: Planning a coherent storyline [Webinar]. National Science Teaching Association.

When they strike one drum, they are delighted to see that a tambourine on the same table begins to rattle and "buzz" and move without them touching it. They repeat this action over and over and come up with explanations suggesting that somehow sound goes from the drum to the tambourine. (This will later become a driver for investigating how sounds travel and what they can travel through—part of their quest to answer the larger question of why their class was noisy to the group next door.)

Children at the tuning fork station quickly notice that the forks shake when struck. As they press the vibrating tuning forks against their arms and faces, they observe that touching can make the vibrations stop and that the sound stops, too. This leads them to think about whether sounds are always connected with vibrating objects. Later, the teacher adds a bowl of water to this table. When they dip the vibrating tuning forks into the bowl, they are thrilled to experience a splash of water. This also raises questions for students about what substances vibrations can travel through—again, getting to an important aspect of seeking an explanation for why the class next door can hear them.

To support students as they make connections and develop their conceptual understanding, Ms.

Kearney circulates from group to group, asking questions like these: *What are you trying? What happens when you . . . ? Did you see what _____ tried? Did everyone get a chance to try that?* She encourages the children to talk about their observations. Because recording observations is relatively new to her class, she asks each group to put away their objects, grab their notebooks, and spend the next five minutes drawing their observations. Then the children congregate in a circle on the carpet for a science talk anchored in what they've drawn.

Children's observations

During the whole class science talk, Ms. Kearney guides children in sharing their observations from each station. She listens intently and says little, except to rephrase students' observations and ask if others had noticed something similar at their stations. The children pay close attention to their classmates to learn what happened at different stations.

After the last team shares their observations, Ms. Kearney asks the children which things were the same and different across stations. Children from various groups start gesturing and talking about objects shaking back and forth.

Reginald: Those are vibrations!

Ms. Kearney: It seems that a lot of people mentioned something called vibration . . . Can everyone take their hand and show me what it means when something vibrates?

(Several children wave their hands back and forth.)

Ms. Kearney (pointing to a girl): What does it mean when something vibrates?

Sochi: It means like it shakes.

Recognizing that the children largely agree that sounds are connected to vibrations, Ms. Kearney asks a question to tease out how much they understand. Excerpts from the conversation that follows reveal differences in understanding:

Ms. Kearney: Do you have to have vibrations to make sound?

Several children: No.

Ms. Kearney: No? You don't think so?

Louis: Because your mouth doesn't vibrate.

Ms. Kearney: What do you think, Riley? . . . Do you have to have vibrations to have sound?

Riley: Sometimes.

Ms. Kearney: Can someone give me a time when you might not need vibrations to have sound. What do you think, Lydia?

Lydia: When you clap.

Ms. Kearney: Is there anyone who thinks you might most of the time need vibrations to have sound?

(Only a few children raise their hands.)

Ms. Kearney: It seems we have a difference of opinion . . . What do scientists do if they've got a question like that and they're not sure of the answer?

Angela: They try to figure it out.

Ms. Kearney: Guess what? That's what we are going to do. We are going to be scientists and design some investigations. We're going to do some thinking time first. If we're going to make some tests to see if we need vibrations,

how might we go about doing that? What might we test and how might we test it?

Continuing the investigations

For the next several minutes, students make suggestions about what to test, how to go about investigating, and how to record observations in their notebooks. For example, some children propose using squiggly lines around an object to indicate that it's vibrating. Ms. Kearney records their ideas, including any new questions that have emerged, on a chart.

In the next round of investigation, students test objects from all the stations, as well as some new ones. Chatting all the while, they look for patterns associated with vibrations and sound. Ms. Kearney circulates among the groups, listening to the discussions and asking questions.

Across the next few days, Ms. Kearney reviews the observations the students recorded in their notebooks, as well as a chart the class made about how to test for the relationship between vibrations and sound, and her own notes about children's ideas and questions. She is pleased to see that many of the children's ideas map onto the disciplinary core ideas for the science unit on sound. For example, children have noticed that objects close to a loud sound also start to vibrate. She thinks about how she can draw on observations like this to plan further investigations in which students will explore how sound travels through materials—and use their growing knowledge of sound to return to the problem of the "loud" class. Eventually, she envisions a culminating event in which her class shares what they have learned and presents their investigation processes and solutions to the class next door.

Inspiration board: Learning from the case

The case of the "too loud" class shows several ways in which you might use a compelling phenomenon to draw out children's questions, introduce them to the process of investigation, and involve them in planning, conducting, and analyzing their investigations. It also illustrates how you might subtly structure investigative activities and guide young children toward learning disciplinary core ideas in the science curriculum.

- **The teacher seizes on a real event to get children's attention and create a meaningful learning opportunity.** Ms. Kearney leverages the children's strong feelings and questions about the noise complaint to encourage them to wonder about the phenomenon of how sound travels. The phenomenon is directly relevant to their lives. They are motivated to figure it out because they are trying to address a problem that matters to them.

- **Children in first grade are capable of suggesting explanations, planning and doing investigations, and working collaboratively.** The students in Ms. Kearney's class share responsibility for learning. The teacher calls on many different children during class discussions, and their questions and ideas form the basis for the investigations of sound. Their group discussions and collaborative investigations help them elaborate on each other's ideas and see patterns.

- **The teacher listens intently, observes closely, and asks questions to guide the course of the investigations.** As the students talk, Ms. Kearney pays attention to their reactions, questions, and observations and finds ways to connect productively to their thinking. She holds back from directly answering children's questions, giving them steps or procedures for investigation, or correcting their wording and ideas. Rather, she uses nuanced questions and rephrasing to nudge their thinking and move the investigations forward to reach her learning goals.

- **The teacher uses multiple modes of communication to elicit children's thinking.** During the class discussions, students use gesture, speech, and drawing to explain their thinking. Ms. Kearney does not assume they know what "vibration" means just because they use the term; she asks them to demonstrate and allows them to find their own words for the scientific concept. In addition, students record their observations and thinking in science notebooks; both drawings and words are acceptable modes of representation.

- **Investigation is not a "one and done" event.** The students and Ms. Kearney use the observations from the first round of investigations at the sound table to determine what to change and what to look for during a second round. The full unit on sound includes multiple investigations over several weeks. After the children reach their conclusions about why the neighboring class can hear them, Ms. Kearney also plans for them to communicate their findings and reasoning by making a presentation to the other class.

What is sensemaking in science and engineering?

Investigation and design provide opportunities for children to pursue their own questions and actively reflect on the evidence they are gathering. This process is often referred to as "sensemaking." As students engage in sensemaking, they actively try to figure out how the world works or how to design or alter things to solve problems. They also take on greater responsibility for developing their own knowledge and arriving at their own explanations and solutions. As a teacher, you assume the vital role of planning, guiding, and supporting them in this process.

Sensemaking happens in the minds of learners as they wonder about and interact with the natural or designed world. Children are engaging in sensemaking when they do actions like these:

- Ask more sophisticated or more targeted questions as learning progresses

- Formulate and express their initial ideas about a phenomenon or design problem by talking, writing, gesturing, drawing and/or making models

- Make predictions about what might happen next

- Analyze data from investigations and design tasks and consider how this data and other evidence confirms or contradicts their initial ideas

- Share and explain their ideas and critique the ideas of others using evidence

- Revise their initial ideas and fill in gaps in their knowledge based on new evidence in individual and collaborative work

Engaging in sensemaking does not require students to do all of these things at once. Nor do these actions need to occur in a specified order. Sensemaking may also

look very different depending on children's ages. For example, a four-year-old and an 11-year-old observing melting ice may generate very different questions and explanations, but both children can be actively engaged in making sense of the phenomenon.

Reflection and iteration are also key to sensemaking. As children investigate, they may realize they need different types of data or an additional investigation to answer their questions, so they revise their plans. As new data emerges, children need opportunities to refine their models, initial explanations, and solutions to reflect changes in their thinking. By making these kinds of revisions, children are acknowledging that their previous ideas were incomplete and are actively reconstructing knowledge—which they may need to do multiple times. Revision allows children to move past the goal of finding the "right" answer. Children begin to expect their science and engineering knowledge to grow and change over time.

Students are unlikely to be invited or engaged to do this kind of robust intellectual work if they're taught science with traditional methods and scripted experiments. An effective way to foster the aspects of sensemaking is to engage students in authentic science and engineering practices. As you work out a viable set of strategies and supports to help students engage in sensemaking, you will be rewarded by the vision of students doing vigorous "minds-on" work and becoming competent with science and engineering practices.

---

[3] Group interview, Jan. 27, 2022.

Sensemaking as a collaborative process

Sensemaking thrives when students work and talk together. When children share and defend their ideas with peers and their teacher, they are exposed to different ways of thinking that may cause them to question what they thought they knew. When children investigate and design things in groups, the evidence that emerges from this work may contradict their initial explanations and motivate them to reconsider and revise their own thinking. Their concluding explanations and solutions are stronger because they have been reviewed and refined collaboratively. Chapter 5 describes more detailed strategies for promoting collaboration.

The teacher's role in sensemaking

Within this interactive, collaborative, and student-driven approach, you'll need to strike a balance between giving students ownership of their learning and providing sufficient scaffolding and information. For example, as students develop their own questions and make key decisions about investigations, you'll need to guide their work by asking probing questions and making thought-provoking comments. If an investigation is drifting in an unproductive direction, you may need to ask more calculated questions to get it on track. At other times, you may let them pursue a dead end as a learning experience.

Although these roles may seem daunting at first, various tools and resources may be available to you. Many high-quality curricula provide detailed teachers' guides for managing investigations and design tasks, along with the specific disciplinary core ideas and crosscutting concepts the units are targeting. Some curricula also come with relevant readings, physical materials for conducting investigations, and tools you can use to guide students' discussions and collaborative work.

If your district curriculum does not provide these supports, you might collaborate with your colleagues or a school or district science specialist to explore ways to supplement your materials. There are many excellent research-based resources freely available online, but it takes time to find and review them. Working with and sharing among a team can facilitate the process. Also, you can approach the work gradually, making small additions or modifications over time as you become comfortable with the three-dimensional approach.

Even if your school is underequipped for science and engineering education, you can use everyday objects and repurposed items for investigations and engineering design. What matters most is how you use whatever resources you have.

What defines a suitable phenomenon for learning and sensemaking?

Choosing an appropriate phenomenon for children to investigate is a critical aspect of orienting them to investigation and providing opportunities for sensemaking. As noted above, a phenomenon is a circumstance, event, or process that can be observed, investigated, and explained using science practices. Often, a series of lessons across a unit will begin by introducing an anchoring phenomenon that motivates children to wonder and ask questions. Students then engage in a series of investigations that are related to and help them understand the anchoring phenomenon. For example, as in the case of the "too loud" classroom, the anchoring phenomenon was that the children could be heard by students in a neighboring classroom. The teacher then engaged students in investigations that helped them explore why that might be happening.

Researchers, experienced teachers, and other instructional experts have identified key characteristics that can help you choose phenomena that might work for your students and learning context. These characteristics are summarized in Box 3-1 and

---

BOX 3-1

CHARACTERISTICS OF SUITABLE PHENOMENA FOR INSTRUCTION

- Are interesting and puzzling to children

- Are relevant to children's experiences

- Are aligned to the disciplinary core ideas, crosscutting concepts, and practices that you want students to use and learn

- Can be observed and investigated over time using science practices and are too complex to explain after a single lesson

- Can be an event (*Why did pine beetles infest the forest?*), a puzzling circumstance (*Why isn't rainwater salty?*), or a natural process that evokes wonder (*How did the solar system form?*)

- Touch upon issues of equity and justice

Source: Adapted from Penuel, W. R., & Bell, P. (2016, March). *Qualities of a good anchor phenomenon for a coherent sequence of science lessons* [Practice Brief No. 28]. STEM Teaching Tools, UW Institute for Science + Math Education. https://stemteachingtools.org/brief/28

explained after the box. (Characteristics of effective design problems will be discussed in more detail later in the chapter.)

Interesting and puzzling to children

As described in Chapter 2, children are naturally curious from an early age about how the world works. When they encounter a thing or event that they don't understand, they want to figure it out. An effective phenomenon is puzzling or counterintuitive to children. It activates their curiosity and desire to understand, motivating them to ask questions that set the stage for sensemaking. Here are a few examples of interesting phenomena:

- **Community:** One area of our town is prone to flooding, while other areas are not.

- **Family life:** Dario's family's apartment on the fourth floor of the building is much warmer than Min's on the first floor.

- **Everyday experience:** When I put ice in any drink, the ice always pops to the top.

Relevant to children's lives

A phenomenon for investigation doesn't have to be flashy. Often the phenomena that interest children the most are those that connect with their families, classroom, or community. When children pursue their own questions and issues that matter to their lives, investigation becomes meaningful. They are more inspired to work over multiple periods to try to explain the phenomenon.

Using relevant phenomena is an especially important way to connect with children's cultural and language backgrounds and geographic location. For example, if you're teaching a group of urban kindergarteners about how sunlight warms the surface of the Earth, you might choose to have them observe hot concrete instead of hot sand.[4] If you're exploring ecosystems, you might choose a desert landscape if your school is in Arizona, whereas you might focus on ocean systems if you're located in Maine.

Aligned to the ideas and practices children are expected to learn and use

A useful phenomenon can be explained with the disciplinary core ideas that your students are expected to learn and be able to use for their grade span, based on the NGSS or similar state standards. You will benefit from knowing the disciplinary core ideas for your grade, and also from considering what your students learned in a previous grade and will need to learn to be ready for the next grade.

---

4 Using phenomena in NGSS-designed lessons and units, https://www.nextgenscience.org/resources/phenomena

> One way we make science equitable is for students to see themselves in science, and science in their world. So this idea of relevant phenomena is very powerful. Look, the Grand Canyon is cool. There's nothing wrong with bringing that in sometimes. But if everything you do is something your students have never experienced, then science is not about them or their world.
>
> —Stacey van der Veen, founder of Leadership in Science and professional development provider[5]

For example, by the end of grade 5, students are expected to know that animals receive different types of information through their senses, process the information in their brains, and respond to the information in different ways. This idea is best taught not by telling it to students as one of many things they should know about organisms. Instead, you could show your students a soundless video of how several baby shrews safely follow a mother around the terrain outside their burrow by forming a sort of conga line, in which each shrew attaches its teeth to the base of the shrew in front of it.[6] You could then ask your students what they notice and wonder about this situation. Eventually, you can guide them to thinking about why shrews (which have very poor eyesight) behave in this way.

Can be observed and investigated over multiple lessons using science practices

For preschool and elementary science, appropriate phenomena are occurrences that children can observe themselves. In the case of Ms. Kearney's class, the children were

---

[5] Presentation at Leadership in Science Administrator Workshop Series, Dec. 15, 2021.
[6] https://www.baesi.org/phenomena/ and https://thewonderofscience.com/phenomenon/2018/7/5/shrew-caravan

intrigued that students in the other class could hear them even when the door was closed. They then explored making sounds with tools and musical instruments to investigate how the phenomenon might occur. They noticed patterns and tried to use science ideas about vibrations to explain those patterns and what caused them.

Observations can also be made with data, images, texts, and accessible technologies. In the Wonder Farm exploration, for example, preschool children look at two pictures of the same plant taken on different days, say what they notice and wonder, and use a digital app to see how variables like water and sunshine affect plant growth over time.[7]

Further, a suitable phenomenon can be explained using some or all of the eight science and engineering practices listed earlier in this chapter. In Ms. Kearney's case, the students used such practices as asking questions, carrying out investigations, and constructing explanations.

To be suitable for three-dimensional learning, an anchoring phenomenon should be rich enough to not only spur students to want to investigate but to sustain their explorations and sensemaking efforts over days, weeks, and sometimes months. The anchoring phenomenon is the glue that holds the lessons together. Something that can be solved through a single investigation doesn't allow for students to apply the full range of practices or develop more sophisticated thinking over time.

Touches upon issues of equity and justice

Phenomena that encourage children to investigate issues of equity and justice can be particularly motivating, especially if they raise issues that affect their local community. It's also critical that you choose phenomena and engineering design problems that are, or can be made, equitable for all students' learning. These issues are discussed later in this chapter.

What phenomena are NOT

Even if you adhere to these characteristics of effective phenomena, it can still be tricky to frame a naturally-occurring event in the form of a phenomenon that can be investigated. Phenomena are not questions, concepts, or processes, as indicated in Table 3-1. They are not the activity or the investigation itself.

For example, if you open science class with a question like *Why do rivers curve*, you miss the critical step of students coming up with their own questions to investigate. And if someone blurts out the correct answer, the reason to investigate becomes

---

[7] Presser, A. L., Kamdar, D., Vidiksis, R., Goldstein, M., Dominguez, X., & Orr, J. (2017, October). Growing plants and minds. *Science and Children* 55(2), 41–47. https://eric.ed.gov/?id=EJ1157157

TABLE 3-1

WHAT ARE AND ARE NOT SUITABLE PHENOMENA FOR SCIENCE INSTRUCTION

NOT a phenomenon	Science phenomenon
Questions What does a tree need to grow?	Look at the tree in the picture and tell me what you notice. Compare it with the tree in the schoolyard outside our window.
Concepts Today we're going to study the water cycle.	It snowed yesterday in the mountains near us but not in our town.
Activities Today we're going to use your shadows to track the movement of the sun.	My shadow is longer at the end of school than it was at lunch time.

Sources: Wil van der Veen, NGSS Planning Guide, Raritan Valley Community College Science Education Institute, Aug. 19, 2021; Stacey van der Veen, presentation at Leadership in Science Administrator Workshop Series, Dec. 15, 2021; Nicole Van Tassel, Science Phenomena for Your NGSS Storylines, https://iexplorescience.com/science-phenomena-for-ngss-storylines/

less compelling. Instead, you might show the class a time-lapse video of changes in the shape of a river over time and ask students what they notice and wonder about.

How can a phenomenon propel an investigation?

An example from an urban Title I school with many emergent multilingual learners shows how a compelling anchoring phenomenon—the large amounts of garbage produced at school, home, and community—can grab students' interest and drive them to investigate. In the example below, Lily Hamerstrom, a fifth-grade teacher, uses a curriculum that integrates SAIL.[8] Throughout the unit, students ask questions and investigate. They gather and analyze data as they sort school lunch garbage into categories, study a local landfill, and observe what happens to jars filled with food and non-food materials. Over time, students develop an understanding of targeted disciplinary core ideas in physical and life sciences.

---

[8] https://www.nyusail.org/

Example

Garbage, garbage everywhere[9]

While Lily Hamerstrom's fifth graders are at lunch, she sneaks out a bag of garbage from the school cafeteria, removes any unsafe items, and dumps the remainder on her classroom floor. When the students return to class after lunch, they are astonished to find the floor dotted with heaps of garbage. "Why is this here?"some children ask, while others just let out a disgusted, "Eww." This "wow moment," as Ms. Hamerstrom calls it, is the kickoff for the grade 5 unit on garbage which connects to disciplinary core ideas about matter in physical science and decomposition in life science.

As students stare at the garbage, they begin to recognize pizza boxes and other items related to what they just had for lunch. Ms. Hamerstrom gives the students gloves and tongs and tells them to start sorting the garbage into categories. The students begin sorting the items in piles. "And without even realizing what they're doing, they just sort it by properties," says Ms. Hamerstrom. "They put all the cardboard over here and all the paper over there."

As students make observations and sort the garbage, Ms. Hamerstrom asks them why they are grouping various items together. One student responds, "Well, it's a tray. It's also very shiny, and all the shiny stuff goes over here." Ms. Hamerstrom uses their responses to open up a discussion of the characteristics of the materials of each pile and to introduce "properties," which is a disciplinary core science idea. This strategy of introducing a term after students have experienced it in context is intentional and is particularly helpful for the many multilingual learners in this Title I school. The students also talk together to identify similarities and differences (a practice) and to look for patterns (a crosscutting concept) within the garbage materials that they have used to create their categories.

After they finish sorting, the students record the categories they came up with in their science and engineering notebooks. To do so, they think of words to describe the properties of materials in each category. They use categories like "paper, foil, food," says Hamerstrom. "And then we talk about how [to describe] the properties of materials in each category."

---

[9] This example is based on SAIL Research Lab. (n.d.). *Webinar and brief 5: A classroom example* [Webinar]. New York University. https://www.nyusail.org/webinar-and-brief-5; and interviews with Alison Haas of SAIL, Feb. 24, 2022, and teacher Lily Hamerstrom, Mar. 7, 2022.

During the next class period, students watch a video of what happens at their local landfill. As they watch, they write questions about what they are noticing—for example, *What is a landfill? How bad does it smell? What happens to the food? Does plastic stay there forever?* Their questions are posted on a "driving question board" at the front of the room, which gives students a sense of agency that "they're the ones driving the learning" based on their interests, says Hamerstrom. And "we end up answering the majority of the questions by the end of the unit," she adds.

For homework, students look through their garbage at home and sort it based on the categories they created in class. The next day, they share their responses to the homework and write down any additional questions they have about garbage. These questions are added to the driving questions board. Together, the class decides on one big driving question for the unit: *What happens to our garbage?*

Over the next several weeks, students collect and analyze data to develop models, argue from evidence, and construct explanations that address the driving question for the unit. For investigations throughout the unit, they make "landfill bottles"—mason jars filled with items that could be found in a landfill, such as a banana and banana peel, an orange and orange peel, paper, foil, and a plastic spoon. Ms. Hamerstrom describes what comes next:

> We watch them rot . . . We watch how the plastic and the foil don't change and then we watch how the food does start to change. And then at the end of it, we go outside and we open the jars, and that's a huge moment of the year . . . If I ask an eighth grader, "What do you remember from fifth grade," they're telling me they remember opening those jars.[10]

Over multiple lessons, students observe and record changes in the properties of the materials in the landfill jars and construct explanations for questions such as *What causes the smell from the garbage?* They explain the smell of garbage in terms of particles of gas that are too small to see and that move around freely and reach the nose. They also record decreases in the weight of the open jars over time., They are particularly intrigued when it looks as if the banana and orange have vanished, but the weight of the closed jars remains the same. At the end of the unit, they construct an explanation for what happens to garbage by using disciplinary core ideas of matter and composition.

---

[10] Interview, Mar. 7, 2022.

> **Children get so excited about this phenomenon that they have a million questions about it, and that establishes them as scientists right away. The vision is that physically seeing, touching, engaging with this phenomenon will generate lots of questions . . . It's not a curriculum imposed on them, but it's the student questions that drive their learning.**
>
> —Alison Haas, Project Manager SAIL[11]

This example is anchored in a phenomenon that students find relevant to their lives and compelling to figure out. The driving question is not presented to students but emerges from their initial interaction with the phenomenon. Students become invested in explaining what happens to garbage and addressing the problem of garbage in their community.

Now that we've explored what makes a suitable phenomenon to drive a science investigation, let's turn to strong engineering tasks that drive design.

What makes an effective design task?

An engineering design task grows out of a problem, need, or desire. The task asks engineers—in this case, the children you teach—to use their understanding of science to design a model or construct a device or product that solves the problem, meets the need, or fulfills the desire. They might also compare and evaluate different possible solutions.

Effective design tasks for teaching engineering share some of the characteristics of suitable phenomena and also have characteristics particular to learning engineering. These characteristics are summarized in Box 3-2 and explained after the box.

---

[11] Interview, Feb. 24, 2022.

CHARACTERISTICS OF EFFECTIVE DESIGN TASKS FOR INSTRUCTION

- Introduce a clearly defined problem or support children in scoping out problems themselves

- Are interesting and relevant to children's lives

- Encourage children to consider the users and social implications of their designs

- Scaffold children in planning how to solve the problem systematically

- Can have multiple solutions

- Engage children in creating and testing their designs

- Provide opportunities to improve, revise, and retest

Clearly defined problems

An effective design task in engineering is clear about the problem (or need or desire) to be addressed. It also defines the factors that form the context for the task, such as constraints on time, materials, and costs; the expectations for how students will collaborate; and the criteria for determining the success of the designs.

This doesn't mean that you should present students with a fully defined problem and context (although your curriculum may already do aspects of that). Students can benefit from taking on some of this clarifying work for themselves. You can give children space to engage in "problem scoping"—identifying the problem to be solved, the constraints involved, and the criteria for success; gathering more information to learn about the problem; and often redefining the problem once they have more information. Problem scoping gives children valuable practice in asking questions and thinking creatively about problems.

In the following example, fourth graders are inspired by a fictional story to demonstrate their problem-scoping abilities and creativity in a design task.

Example

Designing clever tools for resourceful children[12]

In a fourth-grade engineering unit, a book about runaway children hiding in a museum serves as a springboard for a design task. After reading aloud *The Mixed-up Files of Mrs. Basil E. Frankweiler* by E.L. Konigsburg, the teacher, Malcolm Dammond, asks students to choose a problem faced by the children in the story and to plan and sketch a solution. Their next task is to build and test their designs in the classroom using found materials.

Working in groups of two or three, many of the students exhibit promising problem-scoping abilities. After brainstorming possible problems, including whether the problem can be solved with available materials, Joy and Alana decide to design something to help the runaway children wake up before the museum guards come on duty. "But it shouldn't be too noisy," cautions Alana. "They couldn't buy an alarm clock 'cause they wouldn't have any money," says Joy. The girls talk about using everyday things like pencils or rocks and frisbees found in a park near the museum and how they could get these things to make a noise or vibrate in a box. In their planning discussions, the girls take into account the constraints of the fictional story setting (noise, cost, access to materials) and the practical aspects of finding and working with materials available in the classroom.

In a later stage of the unit, Cal and Reggie are building a prototype of a "money scooper" to collect coins from the museum's fountain; this would solve the problem of the fictional children having no money to buy food. The boys plan to connect a perforated plastic bag to a dustpan using a cardboard tube wrapped in duct tape, so the cardboard won't get wet. They argue about whether to add cotton balls and foam peanuts to the bag to "keep it quiet," as Cal notes; "remember [the money] was loud." Reggie points out that the cotton balls will absorb water and make the bag sink, and that when they retrieve the bag "all that stuff is going to come out with the money . . . [and that] stuff isn't going to dry overnight." During this debate, Reggie and Cal negotiate such aspects of design as prioritizing different goals (softening sound vs. efficiently collecting money) and considering the feasibility and impact of using various materials.

---

[12] This example is drawn from Watkins, J., Spencer, K., & Hammer, D. (2014). Examining young students' problem scoping in engineering design. *Journal of Pre-College Engineering Education Research* 4(1). https://doi.org/10.7771/2157-9288.1082

Interesting and relevant

Like a suitable phenomenon, an effective design task piques children's curiosity with a problem, need, or desire that interests them. Children tend to be interested in situations that relate to their own experiences, lives, or communities. Engineering can also be fun. You've seen how often young children are fascinated by building things and taking them apart, and by figuring out how something works.

For example, one unit in an engineering curriculum for elementary students sparks curiosity and a sense of fun by challenging children to design a hat that is functional.[13] During the unit, children decide what they want their hat to do—protect their eyes from the sun, keep their head warm, disguise them—and how they will know if it works. They then design and test their hats using only the materials provided.

---

[13] STEM Teaching Tools, Engineering Hats Design Challenge. https://stemteachingtools.org/assets/landscapes/EngineeringHats-Supplemental-File.pdf

Responsive to users and social implications

An effective design task will encourage children to consider potential users and the social implications of the design solution in the planning stages and throughout the design process. You can also create opportunities for children to reflect on user issues and social implications once their designs are completed.

Identifying the needs of potential users of a design can emphasize the human element of engineering design and motivate children to persist. For example, an design task called *Help Grandma,* offered as part of an afterschool design lab program at the New York Hall of Science, invites children to use everyday materials to invent and build models to solve real-life problems that frustrate grandparents. One option in this task starts with a picture and brief story about a character called Nonna, who pleads, "Help—I keep losing my glasses! I love to read mysteries—but I can't if I don't have my glasses!"[14] By creating a narrative that focuses on the needs of family members, the task seeks to deepen the emotional engagement of children, particularly girls, in engineering practices.

Zia, a seven-year-old girl, first sketches a sensor that will seek out Nonna's lost glasses. But after a museum facilitator observes her work and asks questions that lead her to consider additional aspects of the problem, Zia decides she can sketch and make another invention that will be more fun and convenient. Picking out metal brackets, a rubber band, and other hardware, she then makes a prototype of a "robot glasses fetcher" with "legs" that will bring the glasses back to Nonna. She adds ears and a tail to make it look like a pet.

The social implications of a design, such as accessibility, sustainability, and ethics, are also important. You might encourage children to consider questions like these: *Who will be able to access your design and who might have problems with accessibility? Is your design made from materials that are sustainable or harmful to the environment? Who would be helped and harmed by your proposed solution? What are the risks?* Although children's specific designs or models created in class may be constrained by available materials and other factors, these kinds of questions create opportunities for discussions about the impact of engineering design decisions on people, animals, plants, and the environment. These discussions can lead to design tasks ranging from developing a way to safely get rid of an invasive species in a local natural area to designing a cover for a portable wheelchair ramp.[15]

---

[14] Letourneau, S. M., & Bennett, D. (2020), Using narratives to evoke empathy and support girls' engagement in engineering, *Connected Science Learning, 3*(3). https://www.nsta.org/connected-science-learning/connected-science-learning-july-september-2020/using-narratives-evoke

[15] https://www.teachengineering.org/makerchallenges/view/uof-2493-freewheeling-friction-design-challenge and https://eiestore.com/invasive-species-unit.html

Multiple solutions

Real world problems that an engineer might face are likely to be open-ended. As a result, there will be many ways to solve a design task. An effective design task in the classroom should also have the potential for multiple solutions. Children are often motivated by the opportunity to design their own unique solution. In addition, comparing and discussing different solutions provides a powerful learning opportunity.

One way to encourage multiple solutions is to provide children with different kinds of materials to use in solving a problem. For example, you can guide students in designing the lighting system for a performance during a school dance. Children have access to two different size mirrors along with index cards, craft sticks, binder clips, string, tape, and pipe cleaners. As they work through designing the lighting stage within a cardboard box, they will need to make decisions about how many mirrors to use and the positioning of the mirrors. They will also need to make decisions about whether they will hang, prop, or adhere the mirrors to the box and at what heights within the box. The flexibility within this design task and the opportunity for multiple decisions points allows for a range of solutions to be developed.[16]

Scaffolding for planning

The goal of a design task is to help children learn the disciplinary core ideas and practices of engineering. To make that happen, an effective design task begins with a systematic plan for solving the problem—in other words, with an engineering design process. But this doesn't mean that you present students with a fully fleshed out plan. Rather, your role is to provide scaffolding to help children co-create a plan.

This often involves guiding children in making choices about how they will address the task, what materials they will use in their designs, and how they deal with the constraints and criteria. This planning stage is also a good time to encourage children to think about who will use the designs and what the social implications are. Design tasks often require scientific knowledge to solve successfully, so you may need to provide scaffolding for children to learn and use the necessary science disciplinary core ideas. For example, to design toy cars, children need to understand push and pull; to design a noisemaker, they need to understand how sound is produced—even if they don't realize that's what they're exploring.

---

[16] Cunningham, C. M., & Kelly, G. J. (2019). Collective reasoning in elementary engineering education. In E. Manalo (Ed.), *Deeper learning, dialogic learning, and critical thinking: Research-based strategies for the classroom* (pp. 339–355). Routledge.

Opportunities to create and test designs

An effective engineering design task includes opportunities for children to create and test designs and collect data from their tests that will be used to improve their designs, or to compare and evaluate given solutions. Part of your role is to help children understand that there are multiple ways to successfully solve the problem they have targeted. Children will also need to ensure that their methods of testing will yield information that will allow them to evaluate the design against the predetermined criteria for success. For example, in a task to design a filter to purify dirty water, students need to decide how to determine whether a filter is working.[17] The testing criteria might include how the water looks before and after it is filtered, how long it takes all the water to move through the filter, and whether the filter is reusable.

Opportunities to improve and retest

Like science investigation, engineering design is an iterative process, not a rigid method. Students will need to use data from initial testing and other sources to improve, revise, or redo a design, and then to test the revamped design. The process requires multiple cycles of design, and the order will vary based on the nature of the problem and other factors.

Along the way, some designs will fail. You can help children learn that failure is a constructive part of the design process. Every engineer has experienced and learned from failure. When students analyze why something didn't work and then take steps to address the flaws in their ideas or design, they are engaging in authentic engineering practices.

Meaningful design problems

You may find it challenging to select meaningful problems for engineering design tasks that are accessible to children and are not too contrived. It's important for students' learning to be grounded in situations or problems that people want to change.

[17] The Dirty Water Project https://www.teachengineering.org/activities/view/cub_environ_lesson06_activity2

TABLE 3-2

WHAT ARE AND ARE NOT EFFECTIVE DESIGN PROBLEMS

Move away from	Move toward
Build a dam out of popsicle sticks.	A spot in my garden floods every time it rains.
Design a pollinator out of pipe cleaners to see who can transfer the most pollen.	Our trees aren't producing fruit anymore.
Build the tallest structure possible out of paper and tape.	Children get too hot on a sunny playground.
Design a ramp to make a toy car go as quickly as possible.	People get hurt in car crashes when brakes fail on steep mountain roads.

Source: Adapted from NextGenScience. (2021). *Problems with problems: improving the design of problem-driven science and engineering instruction.* WestEd. https://www.nextgenscience.org/sites/default/files/resource/files/Problems%20with%20Problems.pdf

Designing a solution to a meaningful problem is different from designing something for the sake of a competition or a construction project. Table 3-2 provides some suggestions for making the shift to meaningful design problems.

What does engineering design look like in preschool and elementary classrooms?

A unit from an engineering curriculum[18] for preK–8 illustrates how first graders are motivated to take on a problem that many children can relate to—falling asleep in a room shared with another child. This task is designed to help children learn, among other things, that objects can be seen only if light illuminates them and that some materials allow light to pass through them, while others allow only some light through or block out all light.

As you read the case below, notice how the task and the instruction introduce children to core science ideas about light at the same time children are learning to use engineering practices.

---

[18] Youth Engineering Solutions https://youthengineeringsolutions.org/curricula/

I like my nightlight on but he likes it darker! A design task for young learners[19]

Yazmin was fearless on the monkey bars, had confidence on stage, and didn't run from spiders. But Yazmin was afraid of one thing . . . the dark . . . Luckily, she had a nightlight.

This excerpt from a story called A *Bright Light* introduces the first lesson of a first-grade unit in an engineering curriculum; the lesson is estimated to take 45 minutes total. The story sets up a problem: Nasir, Yazmin's cousin, will be sharing her room for a week, and he's not accustomed to sleeping with a nightlight, let alone one that lights up the whole room like Yazmin's does. Yazmin's father encourages her to consider Nasir's preferences and think about how to solve this problem. "Maybe the nightlight could be bright on my side and not so bright on Nasir's side," Yazmin says. "Now you're thinking like an engineer!" says Papa.

At this point, Tina Chang, the teacher, pauses and asks the children in the class, "How would you solve this problem?" The children offer a variety of answers.

Ms. Chang finishes reading the story. Then she distributes engineering notebooks that students will use to guide and record their engineering work. Students are asked to turn and talk to their neighbor about why Yazmin likes to sleep with a nightlight (for example, *If it's dark she feels scared*) and why Nasir does not (*He's used to sleeping in the*

dark). While the children chat, Ms. Change circulates and listens to them summarize the problem in the story. She asks students to record their answer to this question in their notebooks: What is Yazmin and Nasir's problem?

In the next part of this lesson, Ms. Chang introduces an engineering design process with six phases: ask, imagine, plan, create, test, and improve. She presents the guiding question, *Can we see without light?* (She accepts all responses.) Working in pairs, the children explore this question by looking through a hole in a lidded box with pictures of Yazmin's room inside it. First, they look through the hole with the lid of the box closed, then with the lid cracked, and finally with the lid off. They explore and record what they can see in each of these conditions. In a whole group discussion, they summarize what they have learned.

At the end of this lesson, Ms. Chang passes out a take-home activity that invites students to record how much light they and other family members prefer to have in the room when they sleep. They can also brainstorm with their family how to change how much light shines in a room.

In subsequent lessons of this unit, students work in pairs and use the six-phase process to design

---

[19] This case is based on Youth Engineering Solutions. (2021). *Engineering nightlights teacher guide, grade 1.* Museum of Science, Boston.

and engineer a nightlight that will brighten Yazmin's side of the room but allow only a little light in Nasir's side. Later, Ms. Chang asks students to enhance their nightlight designs to signal whether it is a school day. To address this design task, students develop knowledge about how we need light in order to see, how materials interact with light in different ways, and how light can be used to communicate. Using this knowledge, students imagine, plan, and create unique solutions to the problem.

Throughout the unit, children are given opportunities to learn relevant vocabulary and science concepts (such as *transparent, translucent* and *opaque*) as the need arises. Before they plan their designs, they systematically test how light passes through cardboard, felt, wax paper, and a plastic bag. The task is open to many ways to create a successful design. Students test their solutions, and failure is treated as a normal part of engineering. The curriculum uses the phrase "flip the failure" to encourage students to analyze why their first prototypes may not have worked and how they can improve their designs in the next round. Peers evaluate each other's designs.

Inspiration board: Learning from the case

The Engineering Nightlights case highlights several noteworthy features of the engineering design process:

- **Consider who might use their designs.** The take-home activity and family discussions make the problem more pertinent and further encourage students to think about users' preferences and needs.

- **Learn and use relevant science and engineering ideas.** By working with different materials before they plan their design, they also *become knowledgeable about the names and properties of materials.*

- **Investigate the problem systematically.** This is central to the engineering design process. Students reiterate parts of the process, and failure is a treated as an opportunity for improvement.

- **Encourage children's creativity and position them to act as engineers.** The task enables children to create their own designs and evaluate their peers' designs.

- **Criteria for a successful design are clearly spelled out.** Peer evaluators should be able to determine which side of the nightlight lets out a lot of light and which side lets out a little light.

How can I address equity and justice in investigation and design?

When you center instruction on investigation and design, you are seeking to elicit and expand on the brilliance of *all* children, including those from differing ethnic, cultural, and language backgrounds, and with different intellectual and physical abilities.

As you organize investigations and design tasks, here are several ways you can actively increase equity and attend to issues of social justice:

- Ensure that phenomena for investigation and problems for design tasks are connected to children's particular experiences and lives.

- Give students opportunities throughout the learning sequence to ask, answer, and revise questions. Leverage student questions to drive and advance learning.

- Assign competence to a wide range of proficiencies throughout the investigation or design process to affirm children's identities as doers of science and engineering.

- Value and draw on children's different cultural or family ways of doing science and communicating their ideas and reasoning.

- Allow, encourage, and value multiple modes of sharing children's thinking (such as drawing, writing, and talking) and multiple forms of evidence.

- Involve children's families.

- Use phenomena and design problems that connect with justice in their communities, such as access to green spaces, the health impact of food deserts, or unfair exposure of poor and marginalized communities to environmental contaminants.

How can I center instruction on investigation and design?

The ideas in this chapter are the first steps in anchoring your science and engineering instruction in investigation and design. The next two chapters delve into specific aspects of this type of instruction.

Chapter 4 describes how you can support students as they carry out key aspects of investigation and design. These include planning and conducting investigations and design tasks, analyzing and interpreting data, developing and using models, and constructing explanations. Chapter 5 looks at how you can further children's collaboration and support productive discussion and other forms of communication.

As you find your own style and rhythm for centering instruction on investigation and design, you'll see what a powerful approach this can be for teaching and learning. Children can become so engrossed in what they're doing that it seems like play, even as you recognize that it's heading in a productive direction. You can better connect with children and tap into how their minds work. As the lessons progress, you can see how children's understanding blossoms with your guidance—one of the greatest rewards for a teacher.

QUESTIONS FOR REFLECTION

- What are some phenomena from my students' everyday experiences that I can use as a basis for investigation? How can I make them more relevant and equitable?

- How can I identify local, relevant problems that my students can address through engineering design?

- How can I step back and guide students rather than directing them as they generate their own questions and problems?

- How do I shift from quickly guiding students to the "right" answer to helping them deeply explore science ideas?

- If my school, district, or state provides a scripted curriculum, how can I responsibly adapt materials to incorporate phenomena and problems?

4

Letting Children Lead During Investigation and Design

Once you've motivated children with an intriguing phenomenon or design problem, elicited their initial ideas and questions, and introduced an investigation, how do you move them from exploring to explaining? How do you help students decide what kinds of data to collect, develop explanations or solutions based on that data, and connect their work to core science ideas?

This chapter explores how you can deepen students' learning and engagement in science and engineering practices by letting them take the lead in key aspects of investigation and design. When students have greater responsibility for working through ideas, making decisions about next steps, and arriving at their own explanations and solutions, they learn more about science and engineering than if you had set it all up for them. This doesn't mean that you, as a teacher, should step away entirely. Instead, your role shifts to providing careful guidance and support and anticipating where students may need the most help. Below, you'll find ideas for the kinds of supports you can use and the moves you can make to center instruction on students' ideas and voices.

The chapter focuses on aspects of three-dimensional instruction and learning that may be less familiar to many teachers and students. These include planning investigations and collecting data, analyzing and interpreting data, developing and using models, constructing explanations, and arguing from evidence. Practical strategies for teaching in this way are given throughout this chapter.

How can I support children in planning investigations and collecting data?

The decisions students make up front about how to conduct investigations and design tasks and collect data set the stage for all of the other science and engineering practices discussed in this chapter.

Planning investigations and design tasks

When students plan investigations and design tasks, they will need to be involved in making important decisions like these:

- What to test and how to test it;

- What kinds of data they need;

- How they will collect data and what kind of tools will they use; and

- What will they measure and how they will measure it.

Children learn from being involved in making these decisions, even before they have started the actual investigation. And the planning process doesn't end once the

investigation or design task begins. When something doesn't go as planned, you may need to help children reconsider their decisions and make another plan.

The following third-grade case shows how one teacher helped children plan an investigation of why plants grow in different places. As you read through the case, take note of how the teacher lets students make key decisions while providing them with some structure and gentle support. Note, too, how children become vested in their work and develop a sense of responsibility for both the outdoor plants they observe and draw and the indoor plants they grow and monitor.

Where the wild things grow—and why[1]

For several weeks, Huma Jafri's third graders have been studying a fascinating array of plants—crabgrass, wild strawberry, and Queen Anne's Lace, among others—that have sprung up in an unmowed area behind the school. Earlier in the school year, the children investigated this "wild backyard" by drawing and marking plants that grew in different locations. Through drawings and discussions, they shared their initial explanations as to why certain plants grow in different places. After reading books about plant parts and functions and doing some indoor and outdoor investigations of how seeds travel, the students have revised their initial hypotheses and concluded that "their" plants, as they have come to view them, could have traveled to the yard in various ways.

With the arrival of spring, the students return outside to explore Ms. Jafri's question: *Which places in the wild backyard would be good for a traveling seed to grow and thrive in? Why or why not?* Many children think that sunlight is important. Some suggest that the shade cast by the school wall and two magnolia trees affects plant growth. Some claim that their plants aren't getting what they need in the shade because the plants wilted and became brown as the fall season ended.

At this point, Ms. Jafri decides that it will be helpful for the children to test their ideas about plant growth in the backyard by doing a smaller, more controlled investigation indoors. She obtains some Wisconsin Fast Plant seeds, which

grow reliably, quickly, and easily. She announces, "We're going to do an investigation to see if it matters for this seed whether it lands in a place with more or less light."

Ms. Jafri introduces students to the materials she has assembled for the classroom investigation. First, she shows the children a light box and asks, "What do you think this is going to act like?" Several readily reply, "The sun." Ms. Jafri also helps them identify the role of a wicking system she provided (like rain to keep the plants moist) and fertilizer pellets.

With this setup, students are now ready to plan their investigation of how plants grow with varying amounts of light. Working first as partners and later as a whole class, the children discuss and make decisions about key aspects of the investigation. Ms. Jafri supports the children by giving them an investigation planning sheet to fill in (see Figure 4-1).

---

[1] This case is taken from Manz, E. (2019). Getting a grip: A framework for designing and adapting elementary school science investigations. *Science & Children, 56*(8), 80–87.

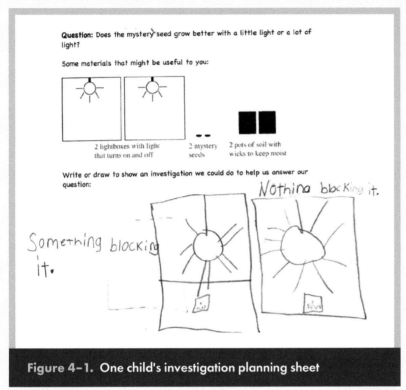

Question: Does the mystery seed grow better with a little light or a lot of light?

Some materials that might be useful to you:

2 lightboxes with light that turns on and off   2 mystery seeds   2 pots of soil with wicks to keep moist

Write or draw to show an investigation we could do to help us answer our question:

Nothing blocking it.

Something blocking it.

Figure 4–1. One child's investigation planning sheet

Source: Manz, 2019, p. 81.

the box by representing "shade." After discussion, the class collectively designs an investigation comparing three conditions:

- The "sun only" condition, in which the light will always be on

- The "shade only" condition, in which the light will always be off, but some light can get into the box from the sides

- The "sun and shade" condition, which will be set to receive seven hours of light per day, representing the areas of the backyard farther from the school wall with mixed sunlight and shade

How to represent shade. The children consider whether they should represent "shade" by blocking *all* light but decide not to do that because they know that even the plants in the shade next to the school wall receive some sunlight.

What to compare. With the focus on investigating how much light plants need, the students decide to keep the moisture the same for all the plants, but they have different ideas about how to compare light. Some propose comparing plants grown in a light box with the light on and a box with the light off. They talk about how many hours per day to use the light and whether or not to block out all light in

What to count as evidence of healthy plants. Ms. Jafri helps students think about what to count as evidence that plants are growing and healthy. The children generate many ideas, including the height and color of the plant and the presence, absence, or number of seedpods. As the Fast Plants mature, the teacher allows the children to observe all of these possible indicators, plus others such as the number of leaves or the absence of bugs. At a future date they can continue discussions of the best indicators of a plant's success.

With these decisions made, the investigation is afoot!

Inspiration board: Learning from the case

Ms. Jafri used several strategies to guide children in planning which variables to represent, what attributes to look for, and how to best align the classroom investigation with the real-world phenomenon in the backyard.

- **Ms. Jafri struck a balance between setting up some aspects of the investigation herself and giving students responsibility for others.** For example, Ms. Jafri provided the light box, wicking system, and fertilizer necessary for the Fast Plants to grow, but she took time to let children to consider what these materials represented. She let the children decide how to represent "shade" in a way that seemed consistent with what they saw in the wild backyard and to determine which attributes would indicate a plant was thriving.

- **Ms. Jafri connected the indoor investigation to the larger outdoor phenomenon it was intended to represent.** Students considered how much light the plants in the shaded parts of the actual backyard would get. As a result, they rejected the option of totally blocking light with a dark cloth.

- **The teacher provided students with scaffolding.** She gave them investigation planning sheets and read books to them about plants. During class discussions, she asked questions about which places in the wild backyard would be suitable for plant growth without telling students answers.

- **Within the overall plan, the teacher left some latitude for students to make choices as the investigation progressed.** As indicators of a healthy plant, Ms. Jafri allowed children to consider attributes like height, color, seedpods, or other things that might become apparent during the investigation. These kinds of differences will likely lead students to reach different conclusions, which will encourage deeper discussions and learning about the best evidence of a plant's success.

Collecting and recording data

The data collected in preschool through elementary science investigations comes in many forms. Children can collect quantitative data such as size, time, or distance; or qualitative data such as observations, drawings, and descriptions; or both.

Although this chapter uses the term "data," the evidence gathered for sensemaking in the classroom may also include information from other resources, such as texts, media, and digital resources. (Sensemaking is defined in Chapter 3.)

Informational texts, for example, can expand children's identity as scientific researchers and support their developing explanations. Media, including computer simulations and games, allow children to manipulate variables and test hypotheses.

Data can be collected in a variety of ways. Students can directly observe and record, make measurements, conduct experiments, and work through computer simulations, among other approaches. These activities can be done by groups or individuals, or both.

Methods for recording data can be relatively simple. If children are gathering observational data, such as tracking weather patterns over time, you could have them record the counts of cloudy and sunny days with hash marks on a tally sheet or colored dots on a calendar. Other methods including having children write, draw, take photos, or simply record children's verbal observations yourself.

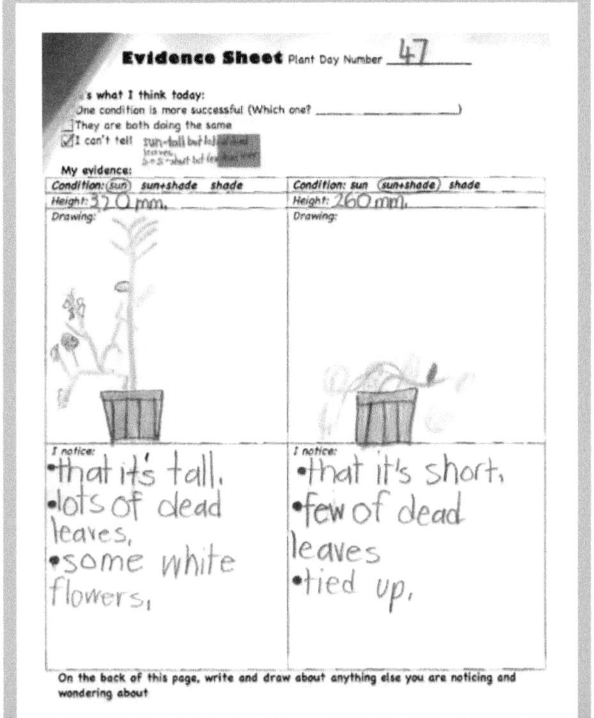

You can scaffold children's data collection with handouts like evidence sheets. In the "wild plants" investigation described above, Ms. Jafri gave her third graders evidence sheets with blank lines for recording the sun condition and plant's height and empty space for adding drawings of the plant's key characteristics and written observations (see Figure 4-2).

Figure 4-2. A third-grade student's completed evidence sheet from the wild plants investigation

Source: Manz, 2019, p. 83.

Science notebooks are another productive way for children to record observations and predictions. Notebooks are a place where students can record formal data and observations as well as informal thoughts and their reflections about the investigation and the phenomena or problem with which they are engaging. Notebooks also offer teachers a window into children's thinking and can be very useful as a tool for formative assessment (see Chapter 6).

Deciding what and how to measure

In planning for data collection, students must make decisions about what to measure, how to measure it, and what tools will be needed to measure it. Measurements are

often made in units of size, distance, volume, or speed, but they need not be limited to formal units, nor do students have to use formal measuring devices. You can use something close at hand, such as cutting pieces of yarn to compare heights or distances, or using blocks to measure area.

Areas where children need particular support for planning investigations and collecting data

As part of planning investigations, children often struggle to design a controlled test. They are unsure which variables to test, what to compare, and which data to collect. They may have difficulty excluding variables that don't make a difference. In an investigation that tracks the growth of plants with various combinations of light, water, and dirt, children may not realize that to figure out the impact of different variables on growth, they need to compare one variable at a time, such as plants with light vs. plants with no light. In a related challenge, children often don't know how to systematically keep track of their trials instead of doing everything at once.

The level of scaffolding children require will vary by age or grade level. Younger children need more structure, but even preschool children can ask questions and make predictions that will shape an investigation. They can also make observations and record results. For example, to involve preschoolers in planning an investigation of plant growth using beans planted in cups filled with dirt, you might ask the children to predict what will happen. If some predict that plants will need water to grow, and others predict that water is not needed, you could propose that they put water in some of the cups and not others. To support the children in collecting data, you could ask them to observe their plants every day and record their observations with drawings or photos. The children would see that the plants that were not watered would shrivel, which could lead to further discussions of what plants need to grow.

You can scaffold these practices, but remember that it is important to scaffold in a way that supports children in learning from their own experiences!

How can I support children in analyzing and interpreting data?

The data students gather is the grist for sensemaking. Before students can use data to construct an explanation, they must analyze the data so they can interpret it. There are many ways for students to structure data so that they can make sense of it. Some productive approaches you could use to help them include these options:

- Comparing the data of different groups;

- Noting patterns and relationships in data;

- Using patterns to answer questions or support or refute explanations;

- Comparing predicted results to actual results; and

- Making models (discussed later in this chapter).

When students analyze data from their own investigations and design tasks, they are testing their ideas against reality. This is an opportunity for you to help them directly experience the full process of discovery and the results of their efforts. They see what works and what doesn't and where they need to gather more or different kinds of data. They also learn from comparing their ideas and their observations with those of other children. Through these experiences you will help children to develop deeper, more connected, and more flexible understanding of the science ideas and concepts needed for sensemaking.

The following fourth-grade example shows how one teacher skillfully guides students through the processes of analyzing data. The opening phenomenon in the roller coaster video captivates the children and sparks their curiosity. Notice how the teacher then leverages that curiosity to engage students in discussion about what their investigations are revealing so far and what else they need to do to answer their questions.

Example

Marbles and roller coasters energize students' sensemaking[2]

After watching a short video of a roller coaster cart moving along a track through loops, inclines, and drops, the fourth-grade students in Cami Padilla's class collectively generate this question: *How does the roller coaster have enough "power" to go all the way?* This activity is part of a unit on energy.

To help students answer their initial question, Ms. Padilla introduces a semi-structured investigation in which students roll marbles down long tracks made from pipe insulation. To incrementally adjust the height of the starting point, students add dictionaries underneath the ramps. They measure how far the marbles roll at each height. Ms. Padilla's goal is to support students in making sense of the cause-effect relationships between the height of a ramp (measured in dictionaries) and the rolling of a marble down the ramp. The students record their data on a table Ms. Padilla has given them, which includes entries for the height of the ramp and the distance the marble travels. However, she has not set strict criteria for how they collect the data.

The day after the investigation, the students review the data they have recorded, with guidance from the teacher to look for patterns. Ms. Padilla spurs their small-group discussions with this query: "What claims can you make from the data to address the question of the impact of the height of the track on the distance the marble rolled?" As she circulates, listens, and asks more questions, Ms. Padilla recognizes that some groups of students are including both distance and speed in their discussion, while others are focusing only on distance.

She brings the class together and intentionally invites students to share examples of differing claims, as in these excerpts:

> **Mia:** The marble went further each time.
>
> **Ms. Padilla:** Does anybody agree with [Mia]?

---

[2] The example comes from Zembal-Saul, C., & Hershberger, K. (2020). Positioning students at the center of sensemaking: Productive grappling with data. In E. A. Davis, C. Zembal-Saul, & S. M. Kademian (Eds.), *Sensemaking in elementary science: Supporting teacher learning.* Routledge.

Caden: It goes faster and further as we added more dictionaries.

Ms. Padilla: Do you guys agree with her? She says that it went faster and further as the height increased. What are your thoughts on that?

Mia: We don't know for sure if it rolled faster, but we just saw that it went further each time.

Ms. Padilla: Why are you saying we don't know for sure?

Lincoln: Because we didn't use a stopwatch or one of those things that can detect the amount of speed it went.

As the conversation continues, Ms. Padilla asks more students to share what their data showed. Soon, the children agree that their initial investigation showed only that the marble traveled farther as the height of the track increased and didn't address the speed of the marble. The teacher allows the students to keep talking, with the goal that they will recognize that they need to test some of their claims about speed. This presents an iterative opportunity to revisit their investigation.

From these small and whole group discussions regarding initial data interpretation, the class crafts a new question: *How does the height of the roller coaster affect how fast the marble goes?* This leads them to design another investigation in which they time the speed of the marble. Students are divided about whether to stop timing when the marble stops rolling or when it reaches the end of the ramp. As they talk through this issue, several students draw on the whiteboard to make their thinking visible. After more discussion, they figure out a way to stop the marble and set a common distance for their time measurement. They also revise their table for data collection. Looking back at the data from the first investigation, many children predict that the marble will go faster as the top of the ramp is raised higher.

The next day, the students conduct this investigation and go through another round of data analysis. Using the evidence, they negotiate this claim: *As we increased the height at the top of the track, the marble went faster.* At this point, Ms. Padilla introduces the scientific idea that speed is the distance traveled per unit of time. Students then begin to ask questions about *why* the height of the track influenced the distance and speed of the marble. As a result of their investigation and data analysis, the children are now eager to develop an explanation.

The rolling marbles example illustrates strategies you might use to solicit students' input and support them in analyzing the findings of their investigations—all with the goal of advancing their sensemaking:

- Provide scaffolding through data recording sheets, while actively encouraging students to determine how to generate, record, and analyze data

- Give them opportunities to decide which variables to record and what claims the data allow them to make

- Strive to not directly contradict or agree with students' claims but instead call attention to contrasting ideas to spur discussion

Through these discussions, you can help students to see data patterns and relationships among variables. You can encourage them to investigate further, reconsider their claims, and start thinking about scientific explanations.

Strategies for helping students analyze and interpret data

Children often need support in interpreting and analyzing data. The formats for representing data can help students see patterns, make comparisons, and do other analyses. You'll need to consider which kind of format works best to accomplish the purpose of an investigation.

Many teachers use basic tally charts to summarize data from the whole class and support students in interpreting their data. Figure 4-3 shows an example of such a chart from a second-grade investigation of how wind and water can change dunes. Using a model "dune" made by pouring sand into a deep pan and adding a cup of water, the children blew air through straws against the dune to simulate wind and tilted the pan to simulate waves. After the investigation, during a whole-class discussion, teacher Grace Hernandez summarized the results with hash marks on a tally chart. This helped the students see that the wind made the sand move up the model dune and

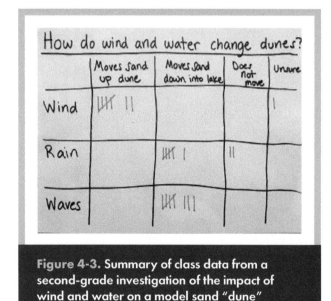

Figure 4-3. Summary of class data from a second-grade investigation of the impact of wind and water on a model sand "dune"

Source: Bismack et al., 2020, p. 39.

the water washed the sand into the model lake.[3]

While these kinds of data tables and charts are accessible to children and effective for finding patterns, organizing charts can pose a challenge for teachers and students. Without structure, the data can get "jumbled," making it hard to analyze. With a little planning, you can help create a format that helps the patterns jump out at children.

Imagine, for example, that your class is planning to plant flowers in the school garden but the seeds get mixed up. Students can begin sorting the seeds into piles by size, shape, and color. Once they have agreed on groupings, it is time to plant the seeds and see how they grow over the next few weeks. However, children may struggle with the complexity of the data—there are four different types of seeds with multiple samples of each. To help students identify patterns, you can plant each type of seed in a separate column of a planting tray with three samples of the same type in each cell. You can then create a large data table that mirrors the planting tray as in Figure 4-4.

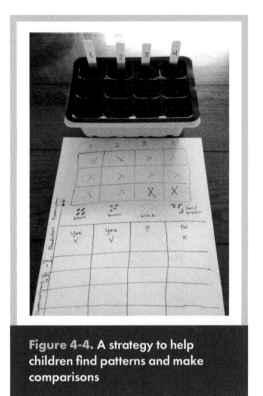

Figure 4-4. A strategy to help children find patterns and make comparisons

Source: C. Zembal-Saul, personal communication.

Mathematics and scientific data analysis

Analyzing data offers opportunities for children to engage in another science and engineering practice—using mathematics and computational thinking. You can deepen children's understanding of science or engineering *and* mathematics through various types of data analyses. In the wild backyard case described earlier in this chapter, students added up numbers of seedpods. In an engineering task to design a model windmill, students used multiplication to calculate the area of the blades in their windmill prototypes.[4] When students are getting ready to analyze data, you could

---

[3] Bismack, A. S., West, J., Wright, T. S., & Gotwals, A. W. (2020). Science and literacy team-up to support young children: SOLID Start science curriculum materials. *MSTA Journal, 65*(1), 33–42.

[4] Manz, E. (2019). Getting a grip: A framework for designing and adapting elementary school science investigations. *Science & Children, 56*(8), 80–87.

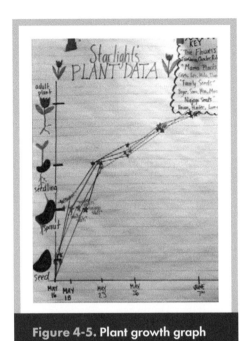

Figure 4-5. Plant growth graph for preschool

Source: Dominguez et al., 2023.

include a mini-lesson to reinforce mathematics learning—a more immediate and relevant alternative to giving them a math worksheet.

Having students create graphs to record data during investigations and design work strengthens their scientific reasoning and mathematics skills. More importantly, as discussed in Chapter 7, graphs can support students' sensemaking by helping them aggregate results across cases and identify patterns.

Preschool teacher Daniel Kim used a large graph to track children's data from a plant growth unit and help them see patterns in their data (Figure 4-5). As a class, the children wrote the dates along the x-axis and the stages of plant growth along the y-axis. Mr. Kim described "data" as "information that you collect" from observing how "our" plants are growing. Children named their plants, and each plant was assigned a specific color. The children observed their plants periodically and documented the results by marking a star at the appropriate place on the graph.[5]

Areas where students need particular support with analyzing and interpreting data

Some aspects of analyzing and interpreting data are challenging for children. You can be on the lookout for these potential challenges and provide extra scaffolding when you see children struggling with them.

Often children downplay, or even overlook, the most important types of data from an investigation or design task. They may ignore parts of the data that don't fit with their initial ideas, or they may become distracted by observations that aren't relevant to the main question. For example, when a group of fourth graders used a computer simulation to investigate which characteristics of butterflies enabled them to

───────────

[5] Dominguez, X., Vidiksis, R., Leones, T., Kamdar, D., Presser, A. L., Bueno, M., & Orr, J. (2023). *Integrating science, mathematics, and engineering: Linking home and school learning for young learners.* Digital Promise, Education Development Center, GBH. https://digitalpromise.dspacedirect.org/server/api/core/bitstreams/dd63fe27-fb4f-4cdb-b40a-a2c9342de88c/content

survive bird predators, some children initially focused on the size of the butterfly or the number of butterflies clustered together on a flower.[6] Over multiple iterations, the children came to recognize that the salient features were the colors of the butterfly and the colors of the flowers they landed on—the butterflies that were camouflaged were not eaten by birds and could reproduce.

In general, you can support children through any data analysis by reminding them of the phenomenon, the question they are investigating, their predictions, and what they already know about the phenomenon. This will help them reflect on how the data does or does not help to further explain a phenomenon.

How can I support children in developing and using models?

Even very young children recognize how one thing can be represented by another. During play, a rope becomes an imaginary firehose, bushes in a park become a fort, or a line of chairs serves as a train. Children also draw pictures to represent things and can interpret that pictures and photographs made by others are representations. This awareness can represent the initial stages of developing and using models and facilitate the refinement of this key practice for sensemaking.

In science and engineering education, models are more than concrete representations of, say, the solar system or a salt molecule. Models can help children understand things or processes that are too big, small, fast, or slow to experience first-hand, or too old or immense to conceptualize, such as geologic time or the vastness of space. The real power of models, however, lies in their ability to help students explain, predict, and make sense of phenomena. In the classroom, models not only reveal children's thinking but also promote their sensemaking.

Modeling can be an effective way to help students gradually gain more knowledge of a concept like sound waves that they can't see, as the following case illustrates. Notice how teacher Fredi King leads her third graders through multiple cycles of creating and refining models during a unit on the physics of sound.[7] As the students conduct experiments, they add more explanatory features to their models with each iteration.

---

[6] Dickes, A. C., & Sengupta, P. (2013). Learning natural selection in 4th grade with multi-agent-based computational models. *Research in Science Education, 43,* 921–953. https://doi.org/ 10.1007/s11165-012-9293-2

[7] For teachers following the NGSS, this case is not aligned with the performance expectations for that grade level.

Invisible waves can shatter glass? Modeling the physics of sound[8]

"I saw the glass shaking!" exclaims a student as a wine glass in a video shatters from the power of a singer's voice. This puzzling phenomenon—*How can a singer shatter a glass with just his voice?*—immediately kindles the interest of Fredi King's third graders in learning more about sound. After students talk with their "buddies" about what they saw and heard, Ms. King asks them to consider what might be happening that they can't see.

After reviewing the models, Ms. King takes note of what the students already understand partially and what they don't yet know. She summarizes the main hypotheses from the students in a document that students review and discuss the next day.

Next, the students get to work drawing models of what made the glass break, using a template provided by Ms. King with three panels to show what happened before, during, and after the singing. An example of an initial model appears in Figure 4-6.

Over the next few days, Ms. King takes the children through a series of lessons, discussions, and activities, such as using tuning forks to understand the idea of frequency, intended to gauge their current thinking and equip them with ideas to help them construct a final explanation.

One of these activities is an impromptu investigation. Based on their play with a soccer ball during recess, some students proposed that sound travels in all directions instead of in a direct line from the singer's mouth to the glass. The whole class returns to the playground to test this by standing in a circle about 60 feet in diameter and taking turns bouncing the ball; the other students signal when they hear the bounce.

Back in the classroom, the children draw and write explanations of their current thinking about sound based on the information gathered

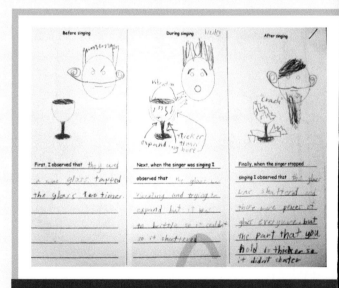

Figure 4-6. An initial student model to explain how a singer breaks a glass

Source: Ambitious Science Teaching, 2015.

[8] This case is based on Ambitious Science Teaching (2015). *Models and modeling: An introduction.* https://ambitiousscienceteaching.org/wp-content/uploads/2014/09/Models-and-Modeling-An-Introduction1.pdf; and Tools for Ambitious Science Teaching. (n.d.). *Using models to develop a scientific explanation* [Video]. Vimeo. https://ambitiousscienceteaching.org/elementary-series/#1479477512386-d45d05e5-57558f5f-0f9d

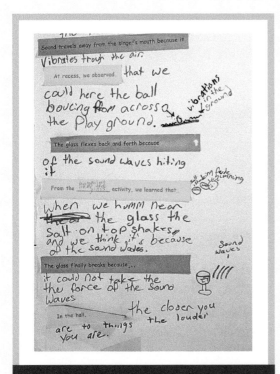

Figure 4-7. A modified student explanation of how sound waves travel and make vibration

Source: Ambitious Science Teaching, 2015.

Figure 4-8. A final model showing how sound energy breaks a glass

Source: Ambitious Science Teaching, 2015.

from the soccer ball investigation. Ms. King gives them sentence stems to help stimulate their thinking, as in Figure 4-7.

After more cycles of investigating, discussing, reading, and hypothesizing, Ms. King asks students to work in groups to create final explanations supported by models. These models often contain rich ideas. Figure 4-8 shows a model in which the conelike object between the singer and glass is meant to illustrate a blow-up of sound energy causing molecules to bump against each other and create waves.

Inspiration board: Learning from the case

Ms. King's unit on sound energy sheds light on how you might approach modeling and related practices with elementary school children.

- **Ms. King encouraged children to represent aspects of sound that weren't visible and changed over time.** As a result, children's models included such features as sound waves, vibrations, and blown-up representations of molecules.

- **Students revised their initial models based on new information from investigations, discussions, and readings.** Ms. King had the students make an initial model, a revised model, and a final model, and each became more sophisticated. (Limiting the process to two revisions helped prevent students from becoming fatigued by model making.)

- **Ms. King combined modeling with other science practices and other forms of communication.** In addition to making models, students questioned and discussed, designed experiments, looked at data, and created explanations. She also had students accompany their models with fuller written explanations.

- **The teacher provided different types of supports to stimulate students' thinking.** Examples include a sheet summarizing the main initial ideas for discussion, a before-during-after template, and sentence stems.

- **Modeling was a critical step in reaching a final explanation.** Ms. King shared the initial and interim models to catalyze discussion and arguments about explanations. Asking children to refine their models after they had gathered and analyzed evidence was crucial in developing a consensus explanation.

The power of models in sensemaking

You can best emphasize the learning power of modeling by having children develop their own models. This is far preferable to showing children models from a book, asking them to copy existing models, or having them build a model from a kit. Models often take the form of drawings, diagrams, or physical structures because these can be tested and revised over time. Many models also include text explanations. (The importance of writing in science is discussed later in this chapter and in Chapter 7.)

When children are asked to make a model, they will draw on their current understanding of a phenomenon or problem. They need to decide what to show and what to leave out, how to represent the main elements, and how to indicate relationships between different parts of a system. The resulting model can be a record of a child's thinking at a point in time, but it doesn't end there. Models are effective tools throughout the sensemaking process. Children can create models to explore their initial ideas, organize and analyze data, and develop and communicate their explanations. They can refine their models as new evidence emerges and their understanding increases. You can also use models for formative assessment, as discussed in Chapter 6.

Models can address equity by offering multiple ways for children, including multilingual learners, to communicate their ideas. The sheer range of forms that models can take opens up new opportunities for all children to draw on their cultural ways of knowing to convey their thinking. For example, in an urban Midwestern district, children in grades 1–3, most of whom were Latinx and Black, used dramatic body movements to act out the interplay of animals, plants, and non-living entities in a forest "food web."[9] This modeling through dramatic play encouraged children to bring their everyday resources into the classroom and recruited their emotions as a resource in learning science.

Strategies for using models

Educators who incorporate modeling in their instruction emphasize several points about using models effectively.

- **Young children need support to understand how models are intended to represent the real world.** To support children in preschool through second grade in understanding and persevering in model making, teachers can first engage them in tasks that help them distinguish between models and real objects or events, and then provide them with different kinds of models to compare.

- **Models are most powerful when children have opportunities to revisit and revise them.** Students can use their experiences, along with disciplinary core ideas, to revise models of the same phenomenon or problem to reflect new evidence and knowledge. Comparisons of models by the same student over time show the progression of a student's thinking. Working with models over multiple lessons can also give children the joy and sense of identity that comes from working as scientists and engineers do.

- **Discussions about how to represent ideas can be constructive.** After children have produced their initial models, it may be valuable for the class to discuss and

---

[9] Varelas, M., Pappas, C. C., Tucker-Raymond, E., Kane, J., Hankes, J., Ortiz, I., & Keblawe-Shamah, N. (2010). Drama activities as ideational resources for primary-grade children in urban science classrooms. *Journal of Research in Science Teaching, 47*(3), 302–325.

decide on whether and how to use certain conventions of representation, such as what arrows will represent, how to show time passing, or how they can "zoom in" to depict a key part of a process or object.

- **A model can be a learning tool for others as well as its creator.** Sharing and comparing student-produced models allows peers to interact with and learn from each other's ideas. As children review each other's models, they realize there are different ways of interpreting or explaining the same phenomenon or problem. The teacher can also monitor what individual children and the class as whole already know and where they need more instruction and support.

Areas where students need particular support with modeling

Findings from research and practice have identified aspects of modeling where children often need additional support. Here are some common challenges and strategies you can employ to address them:

- **Connecting attributes of models with real phenomena.** In science class, children may need support in choosing images or materials that correspond to the important attributes of a real-world phenomenon. For example, in a model of pollination, a pipe cleaner can represent a bee's legs and ground chalk can represent pollen. Some lightweight particles of chalk dust can stick to the fuzzy pipe cleaner, somewhat like pollen sticks to a bee's legs. By talking or working with children as they construct models, you can help them understand how different elements of a physical model or diagram correspond to the real-world phenomenon.

- **Deciding what to put in and leave out.** Models can't show everything. What you want students to show in a model depends on which part of a phenomenon or problem is the focus of a particular lesson. For example, if you're teaching how certain physical parts of a bee are structured to aid in pollination, you may look for a model that emphasizes the "fuzziness" of the bee's legs. But that model may not represent well how a bee flies from flower to flower. You can support children in understanding the strengths and limitations of a model by having them compare different models and say what each one shows and hides. You can guide children to consider the most meaningful dimensions and sideline the potentially distracting elements.

- **Considering parts of a process that can't be seen or imagined.** When children construct their initial models, they often focus on creating a literal likeness. They tend to omit processes, mechanisms, or components that are important to explaining how a phenomenon occurs but can't be directly observed—things like particles, energy, or the passage of time. For example, when making a model of how condensation forms on a glass of ice water, a child may take pains to draw the glass, the ice, the water, and droplets of condensation on the outside on the glass. While it's helpful for students' models to visually resemble what they are representing, in this example key information is missing about how condensation occurs. Students often need support and reminders to think about the parts of a process they can't observe or that occur over a period of time. You could ask a question like, "What do you know is happening that you can't see?" You might futher ask, "How might you represent that?" Or you might ask them to draw three panels showing what happens before, during, and after a change. After additional investigation, instruction, and scaffolding, a fifth grader created a model of condensation that included representations of molecules, water vapor, energy, and the passage of time (Figure 4-9).[10]

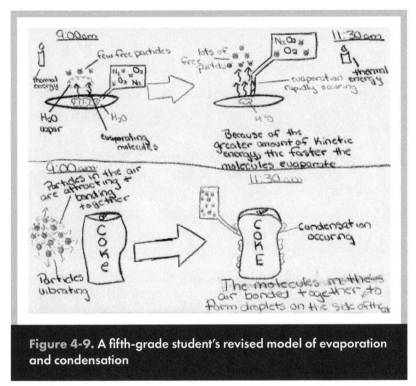

Figure 4-9. A fifth-grade student's revised model of evaporation and condensation

Source: Schwarz et al., 2009.

---

[10] Schwarz, C. V., Reiser, B. J., Davis, E. A., Kenyon, L., Achér, A., Fortus, D., Shwartz, Y., Hug, B., & Krajcik, J. (2009). Developing a learning progression for scientific modeling: Making scientific modeling accessible and meaningful for learners. *Journal of Research in Science Teaching, 46*(6), 632–654. For teachers following the NGSS, this example is not aligned with the performance expectations for that grade level.

Children as young as preschool age can create informative models, with appropriate scaffolding. In a preschool investigation of plant growth, children observed both healthy and unhealthy bean plants. To give children an incentive to observe carefully, teacher Diane Dabrowski asked children to make drawings of what they saw. To further direct children's attention to key features, Ms. Dabrowski asked the children to draw both a healthy and an unhealthy plant. Figure 4-10 shows a model drawn by a four-year-old child that compares two plants, one grown in sun and one without sun. The child accurately drew the "healthy" plant with a straight stem (top) and the "*not good one*" with a droopy stem and "tiny leaves" (bottom). The child also included the symbols introduced by Ms. Dabrowsky to designate whether the plant received sun, water, soil, and love. The child clearly understood the symbols, explaining that "I'm not going to draw the sun because [the unhealthy plant] doesn't get any sun."[11]

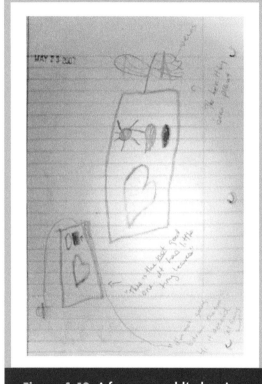

Figure 4-10. A four-year-old's drawing to record and compare observations of two plants

Source: Brenneman & Lauro, 2008.

What are the roles of explanation and argument in science and engineering instruction?

Explanation and argument are at the heart of scientific sensemaking. Yet, these practices are often overlooked in elementary science classrooms.

An *explanation* is a description of what caused a phenomenon or how a designed solution works. An *argument* is a description of how the evidence supports our explanations. That is, an argument is the logical chain of reasoning based on evidence that justifies a particular explanation or conclusion. During the flow of classroom activities, it can sometimes be difficult to distinguish between the two practices because they are so interrelated. Often, students move fluidly between constructing explanations and engaging in argument based on evidence. But it's still important to distinguish between explanation and argumentation. Otherwise, this could put the emphasis on students' arriving at the "correct" explanation rather than on mak-

---

[11] Brenneman, K., & Louro, I. F. (2008). Science journals in the preschool classroom. *Early Childhood Education Journal, 36*(2), 113–119.

ing sense for themselves of the evidence they've gathered. It's critical that you give students space to examine and reflect on the evidence, reason about what it reveals about the phenomenon or problem they are exploring, and discuss it with their peers.

Constructing and refining explanations

An explanation should make sense of a phenomenon using scientific facts. The answer to the question "why" or "how" drives an explanation. So, in learning about solar eclipses, a student may be able to explain how the sun, moon, and earth line up so that the sun appears to go black. In seeking a fuller scientific explanation, however, you might ask why solar eclipses appear so rarely in the same location on Earth.

To construct an explanation, children use evidence they have gathered from their investigations or design experiences together with information they may have learned from reading, videos, or other sources. An explanation may then be refined by examining how well any given explanation fits with all of the available evidence. This step often involves argumentation.

Arguing from evidence

Through argument, children can evaluate whether a proposed explanation accounts for all the known facts, and whether that explanation does this better than all other possible explanations. Often, the evidence that refutes an explanation is just as important as the evidence that supports it.

Students need opportunities to argue for the explanations they construct, defend their interpretations of the associated data, and advocate for the designs they propose. Learning to argue scientifically enables students to use their scientific knowledge to justify an explanation and identify weaknesses in others' arguments, while also building their own knowledge and understanding.

What does it look like to support students with explanation and argument?

In the following example, Bree Jackson's second graders are investigating how heating and cooling transform matter and which of the changes they observe are reversible. In one unit of their multi-unit study of heating and cooling, they seek to explain the effect of heat by baking a cake made of butter, egg, and chocolate chips, among other ingredients. Ms. Jackson uses an unexpected result involving the chocolate chips to begin moving children toward an explanation of the role of heat.

Example

Explaining the curious condition of the chocolate chips[12]

Bree Jackson's second graders are baking a cake—not only to eat but to study. They mix up a batter and pour it into a baking dish. Their teacher takes it home to bake it in the oven and brings it back the next day. There is a lot to observe and wonder about! The batter was gooey, but now that heat has been added, it's a crumbly solid that can be cut with a knife. All the ingredients are mixed, but the chocolate chips stayed separated, kept their shape, and sunk to the bottom of the cake.

To help them come up with possible explanations, Ms. Jackson brings out more chocolate chips. The children agree they are solid. Remembering how some chocolate candy melts in their hands, several children predict the chips will melt when heated. When the chocolate chips are placed directly in tins of water and heated on the hot plate, they become shiny but still keep their shape. Working in small groups, some children maintain that the chips haven't melted yet, and they stir them with popsicle sticks. Their shape changes to what some students declare is a liquid, while others aren't so sure. Those chocolate chips are acting in confusing ways!

Ms. Jackson has the students make claims about the impact of heat on various substances they have investigated during multiple units, including the chocolate chips. As the students share their claims and evidence, Ms. Jackson summarizes their ideas on a chart, shown in Figure 4-11.

In a follow-up discussion, students continue to mull over the ambiguous behavior of the chocolate chips. A student named Sylvie compares the chips to ice cream:

> **Sylvie:** When I have ice cream, it's a solid, but when you leave it out, it starts melting. So it turns into half-solid, half-liquid because it's melting but still solid. If you keep leaving it there, it will turn into ice cream soup.
>
> **Ms. Jackson:** Why is that happening?
>
> **Sylvie:** Because of the sun. But if you are in the fridge or a cold place, it's just going to get colder.

---

[12] Manz, E., & Beckert, B. (2023). Quantification in empirical activity. *Science & Education*, 32, 447–480.

Ms. Jackson: So, what about the chocolate chips?

Sylvie: Chocolate chips, they don't melt as easy as ice cream because ice cream is made out of milk, and milk is a liquid. But it's really easy for chocolate to melt outside in the sunshine. If it's in the fridge or freezer, it's going to get colder.

Other students begin to debate whether the heated chocolate chips are solid, liquid, or both. They focus on the chips' shiny texture and the observation that they kept their shape until stirred. Tony, another student, brings the conversation back to melting:

Tony: So, if there's just a normal chocolate chip, then if you put it in something hot, it would melt, but if it was like a little shiny it won't, but it will kind of.

Ms. Jackson: Oh, so do you think there are different stages of what happens with the chocolate when heat is added? I want to make sure I understand correctly. You're bringing up that it got shiny. Are you thinking if it's only a little, little bit shiny, it wouldn't really have changed state? But if it's really shiny that's when you can stir it? So there's a change that's happening over time?

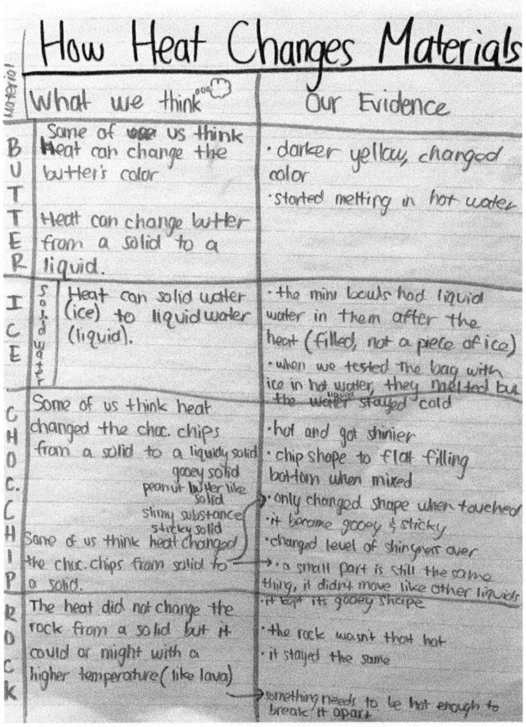

Figure 4-11. Classroom claims and evidence about how heat changes materials

Source: Manz & Beckert, 2023.

Tony: Yeah.

Ms. Jackson: And do you think the <u>amount</u> of heat matters?

Tony: It doesn't really matter because you won't really know how much heat got on it . . . unless you set a timer, for like ten minutes.

Ms. Jackson: So, Tony, do you think it is fair if I write it changed level of shininess over time? . . . So you think the amount of heat <u>does</u> matter? (Writes question on a post-it note.)

(Portion of conversation deleted)

Amal: I know the amount of heat matters because I melted chocolate in a pot on the stove, and it cooked a little bit; it took a couple minutes, but it got really hot and melted into a liquid. I knew it was a liquid because it poured and it didn't keep its shape, it had no shape . . . I know that the stove is hotter than the hot plate because there's actually fire in the stove and the hot plate doesn't have fire.

A few days later, the children consider what they have learned. Here are some of their ideas:

- Daisy thinks the cake batter "was blocking" the chocolate chips because the chips were on the bottom and they melted just a little bit. She compares this with putting a chocolate chip in her mouth, which makes it turn to liquid, probably "because your body temperature was 98 degrees."

- Amal notes that the chips didn't change until they put them on the hot plate and stirred them. The chips didn't change shape in the cake because "we didn't do anything to touch it while it was melting and that's why they got heavy and fell to the bottom."

- Moe argues that "when we ate the cake, the chips weren't melted; I think that the heat from the oven did not reach the chocolate chips."

- Sean explains that "maybe the batter got heated up, then the next layer and the next layer. It got the chocolate, because how could the surface of the chocolate chips be a bit melted?"

Although the students have yet to arrive at a consensus explanation of why the chocolate chips behaved as they did, they have reasoned about the role of adding and taking away heat and the impact of different amounts of heat. They have sought to make sense of heat and temperature.

Notice how Ms. Jackson nudged students to think more about the processes of heating and cooling by asking questions like "Why is that happening?" and "Does the amount of heat matter?" She drew on their experiences at home, like eating ice cream or cooking on the stove, to help them develop explanations. Although some students expressed ideas that were not fully accurate, Ms. Jackson let them pass. Instead, she focused on parts of the children's comments that could lead to more accurate explanations. And she asked them to support their thinking with evidence. The summary chart gave prominence to students' claims and emphasized the importance of supporting these claims with evidence.

> It really isn't about you explaining to your students what the science idea is. It's about you creating a learning environment in which they can construct the explanation.
>
> —Carla Zembal-Saul, professor of science education, Penn State University[13]

How can I support children in constructing explanations?

Children bring strengths to the work of constructing and refining explanations and design solutions, but they require support to do this work. Providing scaffolding is often a large part of your role as children construct and refine explanations. This process often extends across multiple lessons, units, and grade levels.

Scaffolding strategies

As a starting point, students need explicit opportunities to construct and critique explanations. You can encourage them to develop explanations of what they observe when conducting their own investigations and to evaluate their own and others' explanations for consistency with the evidence.

As students' knowledge develops, you can help them begin to identify and isolate variables and incorporate the findings into their explanations of phenomena. They can try to explain the causes of what they observe. For example, in investigating the conditions affecting plant growth, children may notice that plants die when kept in the dark and may seek to explain this finding. Although their explanation may be as simple as "plants die in the dark because they need light to live and grow,"

13 Douglas, J. (2016, March 3). *'What's Your Evidence' Book Study with Carla Zembal Saul 2* [Video]. YouTube. https://www.youtube.com/watch?v=Pgped5maXqQ&ab_channel=JanDouglas

it can serve as a basis for further questions and deeper understanding of photosynthesis in later grades. If you ask children to consider whether the notion that "plants need light to grow" explains all of their observations, they can appreciate that their simple explanation fails to account for why plants die when they get no water. If you encourage children to revisit their initial ideas, they can often produce more complete explanations that account for more of their observations.

Sensemaking depends on children continually refining their explanations and design solutions to incorporate new evidence, insights, and information. You can even use read-alouds to support students in this iterative process. For example, you could first review the progress of an investigation or design challenge and highlight remaining questions. Then you could read aloud a nonfiction text to connect concepts from the text to children's developing ideas.

Areas where children might need extra support in constructing explanations

Developing viable explanations and design solutions is often challenging for children. They are particularly likely to need scaffolding with the following aspects of the process:

- **Including key aspects in written explanations.** A good explanation addresses both how and why something happens, is backed by evidence, and is connected to an understanding of core science or engineering ideas. While children may address one or more of these aspects when they are supported in discussions with you and/or their peers, they often struggle to put these together when they are developing an explanation on their own.

- **Explaining things they can't see or conceive of.** Children often have trouble constructing explanations for things that are too tiny or immense, or too vastly far away or long ago, for them to conceive of or experience. They may struggle to connect what they observe during an investigation with the unseen processes and entities that underlie the phenomena they are exploring. How can you mitigate this? As noted previously, models help students articulate their explanations.

- **Understanding the necessary role of failure in engineering.** Children may be crestfallen or lose confidence when an engineering design doesn't work as planned. They need support to help them recognize that failure is a necessary and productive part of the design process. You can reinforce this with stories of real engineers and actual situations in which an idea that seemingly flopped actually led to a breakthrough.

How can I support children in developing arguments?

Children can begin by constructing an argument for their own interpretation of the phenomena they observe and any data they collect. You may need to encourage students to go beyond just making claims. You can nudge them to include reasons or references to evidence in their arguments and can help them to distinguish evidence from opinion. Students may require support to discern which aspects of the evidence could support or refute a particular argument. You will find that as students gain competence in constructing scientific arguments, they can draw on a wider range of reasons or evidence, and their arguments will become more sophisticated.

Ask children to develop and share their claims

Arguments begin with claims, which are proposed answers to questions about how a phenomenon happens or how a human-made object or system functions. Arguments are built from evidence and bolstered by reasoning. Claims are linked through a chain of reasoning to create an argument.

Throughout your students' explorations of phenomena or design problems, you can encourage them to develop and share their claims by posing questions or making suggestions like these:

- **As children begin to engage with a phenomenon or problem:** When have you seen this [phenomenon or problem] before in your life?

- **As their investigation progresses:** What do you think will happen when we test _____? What makes you think that?

- **As they are finishing up an investigation:** Do you think _____ is important? What's your evidence for that?

- **Toward the end of their explorations:** Let's develop a product (a field guide, signage for a local natural area, a letter to a local official, etc.) to say what we think now.

To reach all children, you should provide multiple means for them to formulate, share, and refine their claims and explanations. Models are a great tool for doing this; so is discussion, which is the focus of Chapter 5.

Although not required, writing is often integral to constructing claims, explanations, and arguments. Children (like adults) may believe they've come up with an explanation or argument, but when they try to write it out for others to understand, they may need to address the holes in their ideas. The act of writing helps them to clarify their thinking. Figure 4-12 shows an argument written by a fifth grader in Lily Hamerstrom's class after completing multiple observations to determine what happens over time to food and other garbage put into "landfill bottles." The students investigated both closed and open bottles as part of the unit on garbage described in Chapter 3.[14]

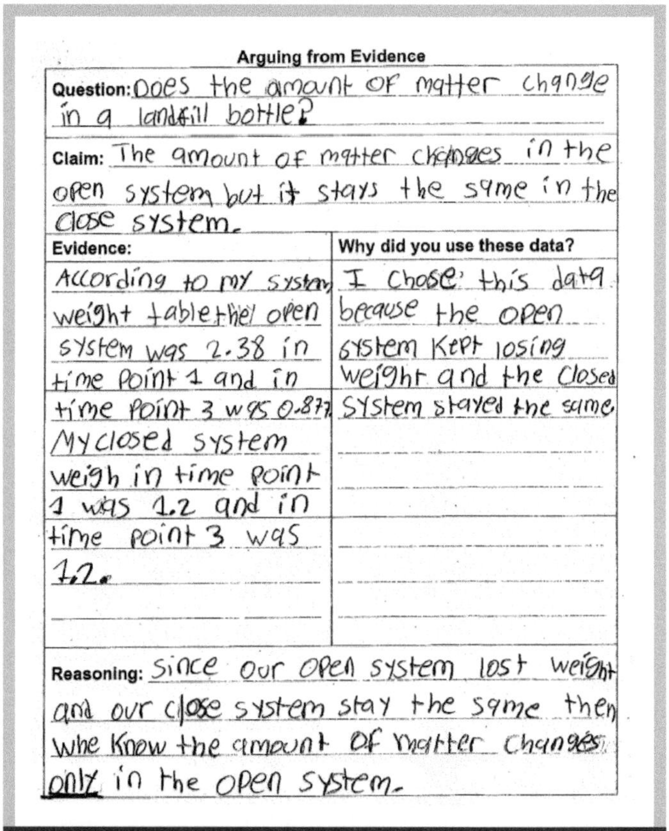

Use a claim-evidence-reasoning framework

One common tool to support children in constructing arguments is the claim-evidence-reasoning (CER) framework. This framework often takes the form of sentence stems that invite children to make a claim and support it with evidence and reasoning. A basic CER framework includes sentence stems like these:

Arguing from Evidence

Question: Does the amount of matter change in a landfill bottle?

Claim: The amount of matter changes in the open system but it stays the same in the close system.

Evidence:	Why did you use these data?
According to my system weight table the open system was 2.38 in time point 1 and in time point 3 was 0.87 My closed system weigh in time point 1 was 1.2 and in time point 3 was 1.2.	I chose this data because the open system kept losing weight and the closed system stayed the same.

Reasoning: Since our open system lost weight and our close system stay the same then whe know the amount of matter changes only in the open system.

Figure 4-12. A fifth grader's written explanation of what happens to landfill garbage in closed and open bottles

Source: Llosa et al., n.d.

- I observed _____ when _____. (claim)

- I know that _____ is _____ because _____. (evidence)

- All of this proves that . . . because . . . OR The reason I believe _____ is _____. (reasoning or scientific idea)

---

[14] Llosa, L., Grapin, S., & Haas., A. (n.d.). *Integrating science and language for all students with a focus on English language learners: Formative assessment in the science classroom* [Brief 7]. SAIL, New York University. https://www.nysed.gov/sites/default/files/programs/bilingual-ed/brief-7-formative-assessment-in-the-science-classroom-a.pdf

As you use the CER framework, keep in mind these tips:

- **The sentence stems are phrased to help children reference both evidence from their investigations and their reasoning from developing science ideas.** Sensemaking involves supporting a claim with both evidence *and* reasoning. In the second stem, the phrasing *I know that because I have seen or done (response)* is intended to bring out student's evidence, while the third stem is intended to elicit their reasoning. That said, for preschool and elementary-aged children, the structure of using three separate stems is less important than getting at both their evidence and reasoning. If a student's claim incorporates both evidence and reasoning, you may not need to use two separate prompts. But you may also need to use additional scaffolding for earlier grades. For example, instead of expecting first graders to write appropriate evidence, you might ask them to circle two of five pieces of given evidence that best support a claim that the class developed collaboratively.

- **It's more important to emphasize children's ideas and sensemaking processes than to stick to the exact order of the three stems.** The framework is intended to support children in learning how to construct arguments, but this isn't likely to happen if you use the framework in a rote or formulaic way. It's more productive to let the discussion evolve and incorporate the CER stems where they fit best. Feel free to vary the order; some discussions flow more naturally from evidence to claim to reasoning.

- **Children often struggle the most with developing reasoning.** This may be a place to provide extra support. As one strategy to support reasoning, you might start with the core idea or crosscutting concept that is a learning goal for a specific investigation. You might then anticipate how you can bring these ideas into focus as children reason about the investigation.

For example, if students are using a fan in the classroom to test a claim about whether seeds can travel by wind, you can support them in looking at how far their seed traveled as evidence. Their reasoning might focus on which features of the seed they think help it travel, such as the wings of a maple seed or the fluff on milkweed, or which prevent it from traveling far. In other words, you can guide them to develop an understanding of how the structure of something relates to its function. Their reasoning could also focus on what's different when a seed travels outdoors. Children might propose that a maple seed would likely travel farther outdoors because it's higher up on a maple tree than the seeds blown in a classroom.

- **Developing and supporting claims can be more meaningful to children if you explicitly connect it to the work of scientists.** For example, you might comment that "as scientists, we can't just make a claim. We need to support it with evidence so that others we are communicating with understand our thinking!"

- **You need to listen carefully to identify the science or engineering in children's talk** and support their efforts with follow-up questions and comments. Preschool and elementary children are generally not ready to explain their ideas using formal science and engineering terms or structures. (Chapter 5 includes detailed strategies for supporting children's talk and introducing vocabulary.)

- **The CER framework should be phased out over time,** as students learn to support their claims with evidence and reasoning.

Introduce a KLEWS chart

A KLEWS chart is a very child-friendly version of the CER that provides a structure for supporting a claim with evidence and reasoning (Figure 4-13). It includes five elements, typically organized as columns:

- K: What we think we **know** about the phenomenon

- L: What we are **learning** (our claims)

- E: **Evidence** from our data

- W: Our **wonderings** and questions

- S: **Scientific** ideas and words that help us understand (our reasoning)

When your class develops a KLEWS chart across a series of lessons, it can also fulfill another valuable function. It can provide a visible representation of how the class's collective thinking evolves over time and how evidence helps students to support or refute their ideas. Some teachers make a row in the KLEWS chart for each investigation (or set of investigations) within a unit to help illustrate the growth in understanding and how new ideas can lead to new ideas.

The same advice discussed for the CER framework applies to the use of a KLEWS chart. Most notably, the focus should be on developing children's ideas rather than on strictly adhering to the format of the chart. Like the CER framework, the KLEWS chart should also be phased out over time.

What do we think we **KNOW?** (Prior knowledge)	What are we **LEARNING?** (Claims)	What's our **EVIDENCE?**	What do we **WONDER?** (Testable questions)	What **SCIENCE** ideas can we use to make our explanation stronger? (Reasoning)

Figure 4-13. Example of a KLEWS chart

Source: Adapted from Hershberger, K. & Zembal-Saul, C. (2015). KLEWS to explanation building in science. *Science and Children, 52*(6), 66–71.

Going beyond CER and KLEWS

While the CER framework and the KLEWS chart are powerful scaffolds, they are *starting* points for increasing children's competence at constructing explanations and arguments. Over time, students will become more familiar with developing arguments from evidence and ideally will not need the formal structure of the CER or KLEWS chart. Another way of going beyond the formal framework: if students are completing a CER individually, you will need to build in time for them to share their thinking through discussion. This can also improve their competence in understanding and critiquing other people's arguments.

Areas where children might need extra support in constructing arguments

Children may ask productive questions and make promising claims well before they have developed an understanding of the disciplinary core ideas that underlie a phenomenon or problem. You can help them to advance their productive ideas by pressing for clarifications and evidence, frequently referring back to their observations from investigations, reminding them to use data to support their claims or refute someone else's, and making time for them to revise their models and explanations.

Elevating equity and justice through sensemaking

Children's sensemaking is shaped by their social and cultural contexts. Their prior knowledge and assets for learning science and engineering have been influenced by the norms and practices, implicit social goals, relationships, and resources present in these contexts.

The strategies you choose to support children in developing models, building arguments, constructing explanations, and designing solutions can also advance equity. For starters, these are central science and engineering practices. So, by emphasizing these aspects of sensemaking in instruction, you're immersing children in the real work of scientists and engineers from an early age.

On a related note, when children construct models, explanations, and design solutions based on evidence, it strengthens their identities as knowledge builders, doers, and thinkers in science and engineering. By emphasizing the need to develop arguments, you also position them as participants who critically evaluate ideas and collaboratively advance knowledge.

As you work with children to design strategies for collecting data and constructing explanations and solutions, you can pay particular attention to these elements:

- Hearing and seeing the science and engineering in the varied ways that children communicate and the different ways of knowing that they bring with them

- Recognizing and expanding on practices embedded in your children's communities

- Building on all children's family, community, linguistic, and cultural practices in sensemaking

- Allowing for multiple types of models and other forms of representing children's ideas

- Making all children's contributions visible to the whole class and highlighting each child's combination of strengths

- Seeking ways of connecting to authentic issues in your community that might help children recognize how science and engineering can help contribute to solutions to injustices

After reading this chapter you may be daunted by the prospect of supporting children as they take the lead in key aspects of sensemaking. Remember the advice from Chapter 1—you don't have to do this at full speed all at once. But, as experienced researchers and practitioners emphasize, you do have to guide and support students all the way to the point of constructing explanations and arguments. Without that, they are missing vital practices of sensemaking. The good news is, as you become more adept at facilitating and scaffolding students' work in one of these areas, it will carry over into other areas.

QUESTIONS FOR REFLECTION

- How can I provide scaffolding to help students see patterns in data and make meaningful comparisons?

- How can I provide opportunities for students to analyze and provide feedback on their peers' models and to revise their models based on new information?

- How do I handle it when students propose flawed explanations? Do I create time for students to reflect on, argue about and revise their explanations?

- What steps can I take to ensure that students from all children participate productively in key aspects of sensemaking?

- How can I structure my class to allow for multiple means of representing ideas and ensure that all children's contributions are visible and necessary to my class?

5

All Together Now: Supporting Communication and Collaboration

Ivy Quinn's first-grade[1] class has just finished an investigation of a "mystery matter" (a melted crayon). Ms. Quinn initiates a discussion to begin moving students toward an explanation for the guiding question, *How do you change a liquid into a solid?*[2]

Ms. Quinn: Let's talk about what we noticed.

Naomi: First it was a liquid and then it turned into a solid.

Ms. Quinn: So we were able to turn a liquid into a solid? Can someone add on to that?

Joon: First it was liquid, and then the way it turned into a solid is that you had to let it sit.

Ms. Quinn: You had to let it sit? If I take a liquid and I just let it sit, it will just turn into a solid? If I poured a liquid into a dish and let it sit, it would just turn into a solid?

Heba: No, because water needs to be cold to turn into ice.

---

[1] If following the NGSS, the example is not aligned with the performance expectations for that grade level.
[2] Example from Bismack, A., & Haefner, L. A. (2020). Portrait of a first-grade teacher: Using science practices to leverage young children's sensemaking in science. In E.A. Davis, C. Zembal-Saul, & S. M. Kademian (Eds.), *Sensemaking in Elementary Science: Supporting Teacher Learning* (pp. 34–35). Routledge. The teacher and student pseudonyms have been changed from the original article.

Ms. Quinn: Is that what happened today? Did the liquid we saw today turn cold? How do you know it turned colder?

Heba: Yes, because we could feel the heat on our hands and that meant the heat was leaving.

Ms. Quinn: So the heat was leaving the liquid? Can someone else add on to that?

Cameron: When the warmth was leaving and it made the liquid into a solid.

Maeve: The warmth . . . you could feel it coming out into the air and it just turned into a solid.

    With skillful questioning from Ms. Quinn, these young children have begun a productive conversation that uses observations from their investigation to start them thinking about a disciplinary core idea of science. Compare that with a more traditional type of exchange in which a teacher asks questions to check whether the students, who are likely older than first grade when they study this topic, have learned the facts they were taught:

Teacher: What are the three states of matter?

Student 1: Solid, liquid, and gas.

Teacher: Good. So how does a liquid change into a solid?

Student 2: It loses heat.

Teacher: That's right! And what is matter made up of?

Student 3: Molecules.

Teacher: What happens to the molecules when a liquid changes to a solid?

(Silence)

Teacher: Does anyone remember the picture in our book showing the molecules in three states of matter?

Student 4: I think the molecules were farther apart in the liquid.

Teacher: Correct. So what happens to the molecules when the liquid loses heat?

(Pause)

Student 4: Uh . . . they get closer together?

What differences do you notice when you read these two accounts of classroom conversation? Notice how Ms. Quinn asks many open-ended questions rather than the closed-ended questions seeking factual answers in the second example. Although the students in the second example are talking, it's not clear how deeply they are thinking or how much they really understand. In the first example, by contrast, first graders are sharing their discoveries, similar to how professional scientists and engineers advance knowledge.

Children benefit from learning with and from each other. In three-dimensional learning, communication and collaboration are the gears that drive sensemaking. As children talk with you and their peers and as they work together on investigations and design tasks, they are jointly constructing new knowledge, explanations, and solutions.

You can use various strategies to shape the context, structure, and progress of these interactions while letting students take the lead. In this chapter you'll find suggestions and examples to help you reach the following goals:

- Establish classroom expectations and routines that build a strong foundation for effective and efficient student communication and collaboration.

- Guide students' communication (often referred to as discourse) through questions, prompts, and other tools.

- Group students and organize collaborative work to promote sensemaking.

- Embrace a variety of approaches to increase equity and engage all children in classroom discussions and collaborative work.

How can I create a positive environment for student interactions?

Talking in class and sharing ideas in groups seems risky for many children. They may fear that speaking out or asking questions will reveal what they don't yet know, put them in the spotlight, or open them up to ridicule. Therefore, a first step in facilitating communication and collaboration is to establish and abide by expectations and routines at the beginning of the school year for how students will talk and work together in the classroom. Chapter 2 discussed how you can set expectations as part of your efforts to create a caring classroom community. Here, the focus is specifically on making the classroom a space where all children will feel safe to communicate their thinking and will know their ideas will be heard and valued while they respect others. These expectations also focus on laying the groundwork for children to collaborate effectively and efficiently, whether with a partner, in small groups, or as a whole class.

Box 5-1 gives examples of expectations for student communication and collaboration, taken from seasoned practitioners and in some cases developed by students themselves.

You can influence students to accept and regularly adhere to classroom expectations by involving students in drafting them. For example, by inviting children to brainstorm about specific ways to ensure that all their peers are heard or that everyone will participate fully in group activities, you can create a sense of ownership and accountability among students. Students are also more likely to accept and follow expectations and routines if you revisit the expectations throughout the school year, asking students for feedback and reworking the expectations as needed.

In kindergarten teacher Virginia Stott's[3] classroom, the children are "very, very involved" in classroom discussion. She attributes this to "my classroom community and the way it's established." She elaborated:

---

[3] Interview, Feb. 4, 2022.

The expectation has always been established—and they have always been given the positive [message]—that risk is okay. You learn from your risks, you learn from your mistakes. And we do that across the board in math and science and reading and writing. That's part of what our social emotional learning is . . . Otherwise, it's very limiting for any type of learning if they don't feel safe.

BOX 5-1

EXAMPLES OF CLASSROOM EXPECTATIONS FOR STUDENT COMMUNICATION AND COLLABORATION[4]

Communicating together

- "We share our time to talk." We monitor how long we are communicating (e.g., talking, writing, using gestures to communicate), take turns, and give others time to share.

- We let others take time to think and find their words before they share.

- "We listen carefully and ask questions to help us understand everyone's ideas."

- Anyone can ask questions if they don't understand something we're talking about.

- We invite classmates we haven't heard from yet to share.

- "We critique the *ideas* we are working with, but not the *people* we are working with."

- We compliment good ideas and thoughtful attempts, as well as communicate when we disagree.

- "We recognize and value that people think, share, and represent their ideas in different ways."

Working together

- We come prepared to work together to reach a common goal.

- We support and encourage each other.

- "We share our own thinking to help us all learn."

- When we're working in small groups, everyone contributes to the conversation and has an active role.

- We value everyone's participation and ideas.

- We build on each other's ideas.

- "We are open to changing our minds" and thinking in new ways.

---

4 The direct quotations in this list are from OpenSciEd. (2019, June). *OpenSciEd Teacher Handbook Draft: Classroom Norms.* https://www.openscied.org/teacher-handbook-draft/. Other sources include Ambitious Science Teaching. (2015). *A discourse primer for science teachers.* https://ambitiousscienceteaching.org/wp-content/uploads/2014/09/Discourse-Primer.pdf; Exploratorium. (2015). Science talk: A tool for learning science and developing language. https://www.exploratorium.edu/education/ifi/inquiry-and-eld/educators-guide/science-talk

Teacher strategies to reinforce expectations

Once expectations have been set, you can reinforce them during discussion and class work through techniques like these:

- Display the list of expectations in the classroom

- Model in your own behavior what a particular expectation looks like (*Ms. Quinn listened carefully to student responses and asked questions to help her understand.*)

- Call attention when a child demonstrates a behavior on the list (*Good add-on, Hosea. I can tell you were listening carefully to what Grace said.*)

Figure 5-1. Classroom suggestions for how to respectfully disagree with an idea

Source: Ambitious Science Teaching, 2015 p. 6.

- Remind students when they act counter to expectations (*Let's allow Sky to finish, Noah, and then we want to hear your idea.*)

- Give students phrases they can use to respectfully frame a comment on or question about another child's idea (as in Figure 5-1); display these phrases in the classroom and refer to them

- Revisit the expectations periodically and invite students to reflect (*"How did we do today in our discussion? What talk moves do we need to work on?"*[5] *Is there anything we would want to add or change about our expectations?*)

By setting and reinforcing expectations, you can help relieve children's anxieties about expressing their ideas publicly. The students can see for themselves how communicating enriches everyone in the class.

---

[5] Quotation from Ambitious Science Teaching, 2015, p. 6.

What does discourse look like in preschool and elementary classrooms?

Nell Wallingdale, a teacher in a high-poverty school in the Southeastern U.S., incorporates various forms of discourse into her science and engineering instruction. To do this, she draws on her several years of teaching experience in grades preK–4 and her knowledge from professional development in engineering and science.

In the following case, Ms. Wallingdale's class works on a lesson from a research-based STEM curriculum for preK–8.[6] In this adapted unit, which extends across 30 class periods, children investigate the properties of Earth materials such as clay, soil, and sand and explore their uses in engineering. Later in the unit, students take on a design task—to build a wall from a combination of student-designed mortar and stones that will withstand a model wrecking ball (a ping pong ball on a string).

As you read the case, note the strategies used by Ms. Wallingdale to welcome and support children's discourse. She nurtures and values the assets children bring to learning from their everyday experiences. She gives her students a voice and leeway to make sense of what they have observed and collectively build knowledge.

---

[6] Museum of Science, Boston, Engineering is Elementary. (n.d.). *A sticky situation: Designing walls.* https://eiestore.com/a-sticky-situation-designing-walls.html

GET SET, DESIGN!

"Good thinking" in an engineering design unit[7]

In Ms. Wallingdale's lively first-grade classroom[8]—which she says may look "chaotic" to a casual observer[9]—she often praises her students for their "good thinking" rather than for right answers. She emphasizes that good thinking can come from different sources—students' everyday lives, creativity, and other resources—and can take many forms. This approach has made an impact, as indicated by a comment from a quiet multilingual learner named Deandra: ''Ms. W said, 'I'll be happy with 1,000 ideas, but I also sure will be happy with three ideas.'"

Ms. Wallingdale structures numerous opportunities for discourse and participation, from whole class to small groups. Her classroom is filled with charts showing children's ideas and comments, word lists, science notebooks, drawings, and books. In addition to speaking, children can express ideas through drawing, writing, movement, and gestures.

Warm paper

Can paper keep something warm? That's the topic of a whole-class discussion during an early lesson of Ms. Wallingdale's adapted engineering unit. In this lesson, students explore the properties of different materials, such as hay, paper, wood, cloth, and bricks. They try to reach consensus about which materials are suitable to sit on, clean with, and/or keep something warm.

The following excerpts give a flavor of the teacher's and students' approaches to discourse.

Ms. Wallingdale: (Pointing to a class data chart at the front of the room.) I noticed that some of you changed your mind [about whether paper can keep you warm]. Explain to us the new thought you had that changed your mind.

Katt: Like, if you were printing it, and it would keep warm. Sometimes when you just print it, it could be warm. The printer might have some ink that is a little warm? And you could rub it against your skin to make you warm.

Ms. W: Wait a minute, so you're telling me you think the ink is something that will make you warm?

Arcelio: It's almost like, when you print it out!

Janiya: 'Oh, Mrs. W! Katt! Katt, you just gave me a great idea! Sometimes the paper's already warm because, kind of like what Katt said . . .

Janiya: 'You know when you print out, it'll print out the paper's hot?

---

[7] This case is drawn from Carlone, H. B., Mercier, A. K., & Metzger, S. R. (2021). The production of epistemic culture and agency during a first-grade engineering design unit in an urban emergent school. *Journal of Pre-College Engineering Education Research, 11*(1), Article 10. https://doi.org/10.7771/2157-9288.1295. The teacher and student pseudonyms have been changed from the original article.

[8] For teachers following the NGSS, this case is not aligned with the performance expectations for that grade level.

[9] Carlone, Mercier, & Metzger (2021) , p. 179; and Mercier, A., Metzger, S., Blankmann, D., & Carlone, H. (2019). Can I build on that? *Science and Children, 57*(4), 26–31.

Figure 5-2. Ms. Wallingdale and her first graders discuss engineering design

Photo credit: Tigermoth Creative.

Ms. W: (Chuckles and nods.) I got it! Now I understand where you're going with this . . . I understand now. So, when I take the paper that's warm out of the printer, if I then put it on me, okay. Now I get the change of mind. Okay, interesting.

Children talk among themselves

Later in the unit, students prepare for the wall building design challenge by examining and talking about photos of walls made from different materials and mortars. In this excerpt from a conversation about a picture of a house with walls made of bottles, three children react to each other's ideas:

Lottie: Can I add something? They probably don't have rocks where they live, they probably don't have rocks there so that's why they're using the bottles.

Arcelio: I can build on that. It's like the bottles are like the rocks in the other walls, but they all have mortar. It's the sticky stuff that keeps it up.

Janiya: Ooooh! I see what you're saying, Arcelio! They're all walls, but they have different materials and properties.[10]

---

[10] Mercier et al., p. 30.

Sticky mortar and bendy walls

The children are eager to investigate. They compare the staying power of different materials by making "sandwiches" of two porcelain tiles held together with sand, soil, or clay, mixed with a little water. Children test the three types of sandwiches by shaking them back and forth on a plate and trying to pick them up by the top tile only. Based on their results, they brainstorm the properties of mortars using terms like "strong," "sticky," and "bendy."

With teacher prompting, students come up with everyday examples of walls with these properties, as in the following excerpts from class discussion:

Ms. Wallingdale: Norah, what are you thinking? What does a mortar need? What properties make a good mortar?

Norah: Properties? Like, you know, you know, like uh, my, uh, my favorite movie I watch?

Ms. W: (Shakes her head no, but does not say anything.)

Norah: I see that there's a tree that has lots and lots of, uh, sap. You could maybe use that as a mortar. Like, get a little paper wall together?

Ms. W: (Writes that idea on the graphic organizer up front. Gives no other verbal affirmation.)

Janiya: Oh Norah! I see what you mean because tree sap is very, very sticky.

Multiple students: Sticky!

Janiya: I saw a spider got stuck in it. And a bird. I helped the bird, but then I got stuck, so it's very sticky.

Ms. W: (Quietly smiles and chuckles.)

In a subsequent discussion, Ms. Wallingdale again uses a question to invite students to consider when a bendy wall might be advantageous:

Ms. W: Bendy or flexible (repeating student's contribution). Is there an example of a wall that we might want bendy and flexible? . . . Again, there are no right or wrong answers here.

(Norah's hand shoots up, and Deandra tentatively puts her hand up.)

Ms. W: Deandra, we haven't heard from you yet.

Deandra: Like the ones that we build from our forts.

Ms. W: Why would a soft wall be useful or bendy? What kind of fort? Like a play fort?

Deandra: Yeah, because whenever we put the cloth it like bends.

(Other children elaborate from Deandra's remark, not shown here.)

Ms. W: Interesting! Do you want to build on that, Jamal?

Inspiration board: Learning from the case

The case highlights a range of strategies you can use to initiate discussion and make students' discourse productive and equitable.

- **Use guiding questions and comments to draw children into the conversation.** In the examples above, Ms. Wallingdale sought to elicit children's ideas by asking a question based on something a child had previously said. She used follow-up questions, and in some cases gestures, to inspire them to elaborate. She invited children who hadn't yet talked to enter the conversation.

- **Give children space and agency.** Ms. Wallingdale listened carefully to her first graders and gave them time to articulate their ideas. She often allowed the children to guide the course of the discussion. Rather than confronting confusing explanations or unclear connections to the topic, she let students continue talking and trusted they would come up with something relevant. In some cases, a peer grasped the connection and "translated" what they thought their classmate meant.

- **Value children's experiences and different forms of expression.** Ms. Wallingdale treated every child as a legitimate contributor to the discussion, while appreciating that their knowledge came packaged in different ways. For example, when Deandra mentioned a fort as a structure that could benefit from having a bendy wall, the teacher pressed for more information, signaling that Deandra's ideas were worthy of classroom time. She gave children a chance to express their ideas by drawing from their own experiences and cultural and linguistic backgrounds. She publicly displayed their contributions on the class chart.

- **Flexible use of vocabulary in context.** As students considered the idea of a bendy wall, Ms. Wallingdale used their word, "bendy," alongside the term "flexible," which describes a property of matter.

- **Support science talk with other learning resources.** Ms. Wallingdale used several kinds of texts and tools to support learning in conjunction with discourse—fiction and nonfiction books relevant to the ideas being explored, lists posted on the walls, and diagrams. Students wrote and drew in science notebooks and contributed to class data charts.

· **Recognize that things don't always go smoothly.** Ms. Wallingdale took it in stride when a child interrupted or created a distraction or when children got excited and talked over each other. "Not everything always worked out perfectly," she says. "There were always lessons where you plan it to go one way and then they go in the other direction."[11]

· **Students add to and build on their peers' ideas.** In the discussion above about walls made from bottles, the children elaborated on their peers' comments without the teacher prompting. Their comments suggest they were thinking critically about what was said. The teacher's message about listening to and valuing peers' ideas seems to have gotten through.

The importance of planning

Structuring this kind of productive discourse requires planning. It pays to think up front about what you want to achieve with a discussion and what you want children to get out of it. This can be determined through a one-on-one or small group interview. You might be trying to gauge children's initial understanding. Or, you might be trying to decide on questions worthy of investigating. It's also helpful to plan icebreaker questions to start things moving and have a pocketful of questions at the ready to keep a discussion on track or steer it in a more fruitful direction. This might seem like a formidable job, but researchers and practitioners have identified strategies you can use, as described below. It also gets easier with experience.

What is discourse and how does it further learning?

Discourse is a process of exchanging ideas and building knowledge through talk, writing, drawing, signs and symbols, gestures, and other modes of communication. Discourse can take place in multiple languages and through different interactions—from one-on-one conversations to large group discussions, and between students and their peers or students and a teacher.

Discourse contributes to learning in many ways. When children communicate, it **brings their thinking out into the open** so others can understand and react. But discourse has other benefits beyond publicly sharing ideas.

Discourse **changes children's thinking**. As children communicate, they flesh out their own ideas. As others listen, they consider, react, and learn from what the

---

[11] Carlone et al., 2019, p. 179.

speaker is communicating. This exposure to new ideas challenges children to think differently and deeply and to expand on and revise their own ideas. This is the essence of sensemaking.

Discourse is a **means for learning the disciplinary core ideas, crosscutting concepts, and practices of science and engineering**. Engaging in this kind of intentional communication allows students to try out "science and engineering talk" through various forms of expression, such as asking questions about phenomena or problems, articulating hypotheses, and arguing from evidence. They may not use precise terms, but you can introduce science vocabulary in the context of these discussions, as explained later in this chapter.

Discourse is also **how collaborative work gets done**. Students discuss which questions to explore and how to organize investigations and collect data. They debate competing explanations, suggest design solutions, and negotiate a consensus, among other science practices.

Through science and engineering discourse, students **also rehearse the social-emotional aspects of respectful and productive conversation.** They get better at listening actively, asking relevant questions, critiquing, and summarizing.

Finally, discourse helps children to **develop language and literacy skills** in multiple languages, as explained more in Chapter 7. Some of these benefits are apparent in the previous case, as Ms. Wallingdale created and shaped opportunities for classroom discourse in science and engineering.

How can I support children's discourse and guide discussion?

There are numerous strategies you can use to support students' discourse and guide discussion.

Start with children's questions, ideas, and experiences

A suitable phenomenon or effective design problem generates questions and connects with children's everyday experiences and ideas about the world (see Chapter 3). Even if these ideas are incomplete, naïve, or technically incorrect, they serve as seeds for conversations that can eventually sprout into the discourse of sensemaking.

An initial strategy is to listen carefully and "hear the science" or engineering in children's talk—whether accurate or not—so you can build on their experience. By paying close attention, you meet children where they are and show that you value their questions and ideas. This type of active listening is especially critical for children who have been historically marginalized.

Try out teacher talk moves

"Talk moves" are types of questions or statements you can rely on to achieve a particular purpose. Purposes can include eliciting and clarifying students' ideas, directing students' attention to important aspects of a phenomenon or problem, prompting students to explain their reasoning and support it with evidence, and challenging them to agree or disagree or compare different views. When you use talk moves, you're also modeling ways for students to talk to each other. Table 5-1 provides some examples of tried-and-true talk moves.

TABLE 5-1

TEACHER TALK MOVES FOR WHOLE-GROUP OR SMALL-GROUP DISCUSSIONS

Objective	Example
Eliciting things children notice and wonder about	· How do you think _____ happens? · What did you notice about it? · What did you notice when _____ happened? · When did it seem to occur? · What are you wondering about? · Did anything surprise you in today's investigation/text? · What do you wonder after today's lesson?
Rephrasing	· So let me see if I've got your thinking right. You're saying _____? (with space for the student to follow up)
Seeking additional information	· Can you say more about that? · What do you mean by that? · Can you give an example?
Adding on	· Who can add onto the idea that [student name] is building? · Can anyone take that suggestion and push it a little further?

Objective	Example
Explaining another's meaning	· Can you repeat what they just said in your own words? · Who thinks they could explain in their words why [student name] came up with that answer? · Why do you think they said that?
Connecting with personal experience	· Have you seen this in your everyday life? If so, where? · What do you already know about _____? · Does the data support your prior knowledge about _____?
Inviting agreement or disagreement	· What do people think about what [student name] just said? · Do you agree or disagree, and why? · Does anyone want to respond to that idea?
Pressing for reasoning and evidence	· Why do you think that? · What evidence helped you arrive at that answer (or conclusion)? · Is there anything in the text that made you think that? · What did you see in the investigation that made you think that? · What other sources of evidence could you use to support your claim (book, investigation, previous lesson, an experience)? · What might be going on that we can't see? · You're telling me the beginning and end of the story; can you tell me the middle of the story?

Objective	Example
Challenging or proposing a counterexample	· Does it always work that way? · How does that idea compare or contrast with [student name]'s example? · What if it had been _____ instead? What if _____ happened instead of _____? · Is there evidence that doesn't fit with your explanation? How could you modify your explanation so the evidence fits?
Clarifying and summing up	· How could we explain this to someone who was not here?

Sources: Michaels, S., Shouse, A., & Schweingruber, H. (2008). *Ready, set, science! Putting research to work in K-8 science classrooms.* The National Academies Press; Michaels, S., & O'Connor, C. (2012). *Talk science primer.* Talk Science Project at TERC; Zembal-Saul, C., McNeill, K., & Hershberger, K. (2013). *What's your evidence?: Engaging K-5 students in constructing explanations in science.* Pearson Education. See Table 4.2: Using the CER Framework to Support Small Group Talk; West, J. M., Wright, T. S., & Gotwals, A. W. (2021). Supporting scientific discussions: Moving kindergartners' conversations forward. *Reading Teacher, 74*(6), 703–712; and Ambitious Science Teaching. (2014). Teaching practice set: Eliciting students' ideas and adapting instruction. http://ambitiousscienceteaching.org/wp-content/uploads/2014/08/Primer-Eliciting-Students-Ideas.pdf

Different talk moves are suitable for different situations. When you're facilitating a whole-class discussion, for example, you'll want to motivate children to contribute, listen, and respond to others' ideas. You'll make calculated decisions to shift the direction when needed. At times you may ask a child to participate who hasn't spoken in a while (*Tommy, we haven't heard from you, do you want to build on that? What were you thinking just now?*).

During a turn-and-talk or small group discussion, you may listen for children's ideas and ask questions to help prepare them to contribute their ideas to later discussions (*Can you say more about that?*). You can also use talk moves to strengthen connections between students and help them build collective knowledge (*Can someone build on what Abby just said?*).

These talk moves aren't limited to large or small group discussions. Some of these questions and comments may be useful to interject as you circulate while students collaborate on investigations or do individual work. In the next example, notice how Miranda Menten, an instructional coach, uses different talk moves to help her students learn about batteries.

Example

Ms. Menten's talk moves[12]

During a lesson on electrical circuits, fourth-grade students observe a working flashlight and learn about batteries. Afterward, Miranda Menten, an experienced instructional coach and guest teacher, manages a whole-class discussion. In this discussion, the students are trying to make sense of how energy transforms from chemical energy in a battery to electrical energy in a wire, and then from electrical energy to heat and light energy in the flashlight bulb. Ms. Menten uses a variety of talk moves to encourage students to share and collectively construct their ideas. The three following moves are consistently effective.

Using a referent. Ms. Menten often refers to something students have said, seen, or done earlier in the unit, or to something physical in the classroom like a list of children's ideas or a poster of an object they were studying. Here are some examples of how she works referents into the conversation:

- But wait, hold on, to go from here to here (pointing at a poster), what made the energy change in the wire to heat and light in the light bulb?

- So then the question I thought of when you said that is, at what point does it change? Does it change to light energy here? Here? Here? (Pointing at different places in the light bulb diagram.)

- That gets to Evan's idea . . . Perhaps it changes . . . like Evan said.

Asking open-ended questions. After one student concludes that the energy in the wire is electrical, Ms. Menten raises this open-ended question:

- What made [the energy] transform? . . . In our flashlight system, what makes the energy change from inside the wire being electrical then it comes out as light and heat? What makes it change?

Using prompts with individual children. At several points during the discussion, Ms. Menten directs prompts to specific children, as in these excerpts:

---

[12] The example is taken from Colley, C., & Windschitl, M. (2016). Rigor in elementary science students' discourse: The role of responsiveness and supportive conditions for talk. *Science Education, 100*(6), 1009–1038.

- [Haile] says that [the filament of the wire is] where it turns into light. How do you know that, Haile?

- Evan, can you finish your thought, then Brooke can add on? (Prompt made after Evan proposes that rubbing a flint stone with steel will make a spark that changes electrical energy to heat.)

By combining the three talk moves in the example, Ms. Menten nudges her students to come up with explanations that require a deeper level of reasoning than simply naming parts of a circuit or labeling types of energy on a circuit diagram. She prompts students to say more about their thinking and to move from features they can observe to causes that are unobservable.

Assure children that it's okay to be incorrect or uncertain

As you elicit children's ideas, you can emphasize that even bumps in the road can contribute to learning. For example, in a lesson on batteries and light bulbs, you could signal the power of "mistakes" by emphasizing that students need to see and record which configurations *do not* light the bulb to help them figure out which configurations *do* light the bulb. Similarly, through your classroom talk, you can help children recognize that "wrong" predictions serve an important purpose by inserting into the discussion a range of ideas for students to test.

You can also highlight the value of saying "I don't know," "I'm not sure," or "That doesn't make sense to me" by showing excitement when uncertainty arises and modeling these kinds of phrases yourself. This sends a message that science and engineering questions start from uncertainty and that the desire to know more leads to powerful explanations.

Promote sensemaking through rigorous discourse

While having a toolkit of talk moves like those in Table 5-1 can bring out students' ideas and generate good discussion, sensemaking is not likely to happen unless children do something with the ideas they've put forward. "Doing something" includes the rigorous intellectual work described in Chapter 4—collecting data, developing and refining models, constructing and revising explanations, and arguing with evidence—

and in the process, building knowledge of disciplinary core ideas and crosscutting concepts.[13]

Research suggests that rigorous discourse is more likely to occur when teachers use certain strategies, including open-ended questions, follow-up prompts, references to activities or models, and invitations for students to comment on their peers' ideas. These moves are especially effective when used in combination.[14] Teachers can reinforce sensemaking by creating opportunities before and after discussion for students to represent and inspect their own and others' ideas through writing, drawing, or modeling.

What other forms of communication can promote science learning?

Teachers who effectively organize classroom discourse set up opportunities for children to use various modes of communication, in addition to talking, to convey their thinking. This flexibility advances equity and opens up more means for you to connect with children and energize the whole class. Here are some additional ways in which children can communicate their ideas:

- **Writing.** Writing is an important part of science, not just language arts. In science and engineering, students write to make science notebook entries, record data, contribute to classroom charts, label models, develop explanations, and much

---

[13] Colley & Windschitl, 2016.
[14] Ibid.

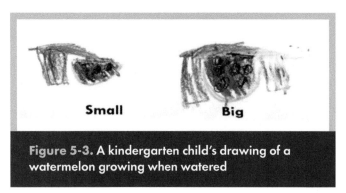

Figure 5-3. A kindergarten child's drawing of a watermelon growing when watered

Source: Charara et al., 2021.

more.[15] Writing and science talk reinforce each other. In the writing children do for science and engineering purposes, you need not be a stickler about spelling and grammar—what matters most is how children are conveying their science ideas. In fact, "writing" may include single word labels or, in the case of very young learners, simply recording the first letter of a word.

Fourth-grade teacher Barbara Germain emphasizes the value of writing in science journals to improve both writing skills and science content:[16]

> When my students first started with the science curriculum, science journals were completely new to them . . . But then as the years progressed, my students have had time to journal since kindergarten. And because of that. I think it's strengthening my students' writing—I wouldn't say mechanics-wise, like capitalization. But the content of the writing over the years has gotten better.

- **Drawing.** Drawing is a particularly suitable means of expression for all children, but especially for nonverbal and/or students (of any age) whose language skills are still developing. In a kindergarten class, for example, a student drew a picture of a watermelon getting bigger when it was watered (Figure 5-3), which revealed the child's understanding that plants need water to grow.[17]

- **Models and artifacts.** Chapter 4 gives several examples of how children express their initial ideas and growing understanding through models that they create and refine and other forms of representation. You can also make available other kinds of physical objects to support investigation and design work, as Ms. Wallingdale did with photos of different kinds of walls and physical examples of materials.

- **Gestures.** In Ms. Menten's class on electrical energy, a fourth grader named Rosie suggested that electrical energy changes into light in the filament of the flashlight

---

[15] Carlone et al., 2021.

[16] Group interview, Jan. 12, 2022.

[17] Charara, J., Miller, E. A., & Krajcik, J. (2021). Knowledge in use: Designing for play in kindergarten science contexts. *Journal for Leadership, Equity, and Research, 7*(1).

"because it's curly-Q'ed so tightly that the energy rubs against each other which makes a spark and makes light." Ms. Menten followed up by asking everyone in the class to rub their hands together and say what it feels like. Students shouted out, "Friction! Spark! Spark! Hot! Hot!" Haile deduced that "it's heat energy."[18]

Physical resources like a driving question board can also enhance discourse. In addition to publicly recognizing all children's contributions, these kinds of resources can help everyone keep track of and add to the growing set of questions, comments, and proposed solutions that connect to their experience and understanding.

How can I support peer-to-peer conversation and interactions?

Children learn science and engineering not only through teacher-guided discussions but also by talking among themselves. With explicit support and modeling from the teacher and sufficient time to get acclimated, students can have meaningful peer conversations even when the teacher isn't directly overseeing.

How can you prepare students to have constructive peer discussions? These strategies can be effective:[19]

- **In your own discussions with students, model phrasing, questions, and strategies children can use.** Call attention to and even name the talk move that you're using and what purpose it serves.

- **Display selected talk moves and remind students to use them.** Some teachers post these around the room, and others make table tents for students to have at their desks during discussions.

- **Review the expectations you've set for civil discussion.** Remind them to be respectful, accept different ways of communicating, and include everyone in their group in the conversation.

- **Help students feel comfortable with giving and accepting criticism.** Emphasize that they are critiquing ideas, not the person.

- **Have students reflect on how they did after a key conversation.** Ask them what they plan to do differently the next time they're conversing with peers in groups.

---

[18] Colley & Windschitl, 2016.
[19] Schwarz et al., 2009; Ambitious Science Teaching (2015); Windschitl, M., Thompson, J., & Braaten, M. (2018). *Ambitious science teaching.* Harvard Education Press.

> **Working together is big. There are a ton of social-emotional skills that can come along with that, if there's any way to make an activity, or take the activity you have, and somehow have children work together. Whether it's pairing them up so they're actually collaborating or if they just have to pass materials and share materials—that's a social skill that we teach them.**
>
> —Jessica Silver, university research associate and former preschool teacher[20]

Getting students accustomed to these ways of talking to one another takes time. While talk moves can be a powerful support for children, as with the CER framework and KLEWS scaffold discussed in Chapter 4, the focus should be on children's ideas and their expressions. It should not be on compliance with using specific talk moves. Give them time and latitude to improve, and they will engage with their peers in ways that they'll enjoy and you'll find rewarding.

How can I structure activities and group students to promote collaboration?

The decisions you make about how to structure activities and group students strongly influence how they work and talk together.

Benefits of different structures and groupings

Different structures and groupings serve different purposes. Table 5-2 shows examples of different structures for students, along with appropriate group sizes, teacher roles, and equity benefits for each structure.

---

[20] Interview, May 16, 2022.

TABLE 5-2

STRUCTURES AND GROUPINGS FOR STUDENT INTERACTION

Structure	Groupings	Teacher's role	Implications for equity
Turn and talk briefly to a peer	Pairs or small groups	Elicit ideas for whole-group work	Low-stakes way of starting conversation Helps build a caring community
Group task	Pairs or small groups	Help students determine task and roles Circulate to support children	Enhances learning by having children take on sensemaking roles
Collective exploration (investigation or design)	Whole group, small group, or centers	Help children understand how to go about investigating or designing	Can make visible children's strengths (even when marginalized in other subjects)
Collective sharing of knowledge and student work products	Small group, jigsaw, gallery walk, presentation	Select and structure student work Highlight connections across groups	Can make visible children's strengths (even when marginalized in other subjects)
Open discussion	Whole group	Serve as an attentive listener and participant	Can welcome a range of ways of knowing
Guided discussion	Whole group	Facilitate Help children relate their ideas to each other's	Can welcome a range of ways of knowing

Although you may have more experience with some of the structures in Table 5-2 than others, you and your students will benefit if you vary the structure and size of group activities and the makeup of groups. Mixing it up will give them multiple ways to find their voice and show their strengths.

Some students may feel more comfortable sharing with just one or a few students than in larger groups. For example, asking children to turn and talk to a neighbor or partner is a low-stakes way of getting them accustomed to listening, talking, and jointly developing understanding. They can also rehearse their ideas with a partner before putting them out to a larger group.

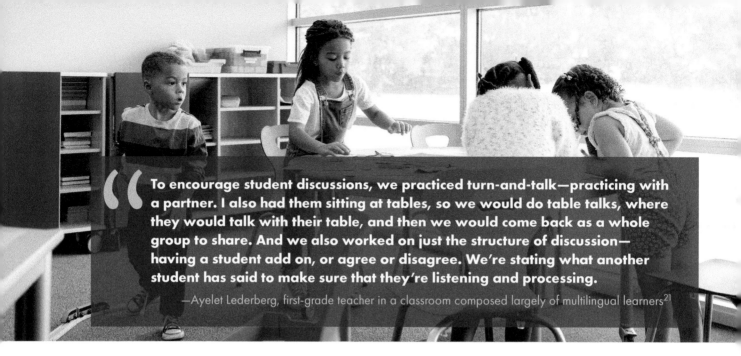

> "To encourage student discussions, we practiced turn-and-talk—practicing with a partner. I also had them sitting at tables, so we would do table talks, where they would talk with their table, and then we would come back as a whole group to share. And we also worked on just the structure of discussion—having a student add on, or agree or disagree. We're stating what another student has said to make sure that they're listening and processing.
>
> —Ayelet Lederberg, first-grade teacher in a classroom composed largely of multilingual learners[21]

Other structures are particularly conducive to building collaborative skills. In a "jigsaw" structure, for example, individuals or small teams take responsibility for becoming specialists in one aspect of a science or engineering investigation. Then several individuals or teams convene and teach each other what they have learned—assembling their separate pieces of knowledge to form a whole explanation of the "puzzle." This structure supports cooperative learning while empowering individuals. In a gallery walk, individuals or groups of children situate their models, explanations, or solutions around the classroom. Then the children move about the room to look at, ask questions about, and learn from each other's work. They get practice in analyzing and critiquing the ideas of others.

For hands-on investigations and design tasks, small groups are often an effective structure. Each student has a substantive role, as explained below. This presents more situations for discourse than a large group does, as children engage in sophisticated teamwork, contribute to the whole task, and demonstrate their competence. Small groups can also send a message that scientific knowledge is collectively generated ("our ideas") rather than individually owned ("Frank's idea").

Strategies for organizing and supporting small group work

Experienced practitioners and researchers who have closely observed classrooms have come up with the following suggestions for how you can organize and support students when they collaborate in small groups on science investigations and engineering design tasks:[22]

---

[21] Interview, Feb. 3, 2022.

[22] Many of these suggestions come from Davis, E. A., & Palincsar, A. S. (2023). Engagement in high-leverage science teaching practices among novice elementary teachers. *Science Education, 107*, 291–332; and Felazzo, L. (2021). What are the best strategies for small-group instruction? *Education Week.* https://www.edweek.org/teaching-learning/opinion-what-are-the-best-strategies-for-small-group-instruction/2021/11

- **Be deliberate in assigning group members.** Based on your own experience with assigning students to groups, you know how to group students with different abilities, particular strengths, home languages and English language proficiency, and other characteristics. Assigning students strategically can disrupt existing hierarchies (*Declan is the smartest engineer*) and reveal previously unknown competencies (*Fiona, that's a great idea for our windmill blades!*). Rearranging group membership for different tasks can expose children to new ideas from more students and give them additional opportunities to build collaborative skills.

- **Ensure that everyone in a group has a meaningful responsibility.** For each task, you'll have to decide whether to allow children in the group to negotiate the roles, with your guidance, or to assign roles yourself. In either case, you'll want to make sure that everyone has an active "thinking" role and in some way is a knowledge generator. It's also important to rotate responsibilities periodically. In assigning roles for a lesson on heat energy, one teacher remarked that "we were really working on being accurate but also making sure that each person had a role within the experiment, because I have kids that will just do the whole thing and the other kids will just sit back. So, I really wanted to provide a way for each kid to be invested."[23]

- **Give clear directions up front to enable groups to work independently.** This could include explaining the goals and basic procedure for an investigation or design task, the time frame, the products students need to complete (such as data collection sheets or notebook pages), and other information needed to make the task productive. At the same time, you don't want to constrain children's initiative and learning opportunities by being too prescriptive. When you introduce a task, it may also be a good time to review class expectations for respectful and inclusive interactions.

- **Circulate and monitor student work.** As students go about their investigation or task, you'll want to ask questions and make comments to determine what they're doing (*Let me see what you've made*) and how much they understand (*Why do you think your bean sprout is twisted?*). You'll also want to see where they are heading (*What's your next step?*) and guide them in productive directions (*How will you make your car turn?*).

- **Set up ways for small groups to show their work and get feedback.** Groups could share the results of their investigations or design tasks with the larger class

---

[23] Davis & Palincsar, 2023, p. 316.

by displaying models or giving presentations, with opportunities for comments, questions, and feedback from peers and the teacher.

How can I ensure that communication and collaborative work are inclusive and equitable?

In classrooms centered on investigation and design, most of the learning happens through children communicating and working together. In the process, children express their ideas in different ways and draw on different cultural and linguistic resources. Using deliberate strategies that value these differences advances access and equity for children who have been historically marginalized based on their language, race and ethnicity, disabilities, gender, prior knowledge or experiences, or other dimensions of identity. These strategies, which are described below, also enrich learning for all children by bringing out a broader range of ideas, assets, and ways to connect with science and engineering.

Welcome multiple forms of expression

As noted earlier in this chapter, embracing both verbal and non-verbal forms of expression increases opportunities for all children to communicate their thinking. Children who are hesitant to speak out for any number of reasons can often do better if they write, draw, gesture, or model ideas. For children with disabilities, this kind of flexibility is critical to accommodate their learning needs, as the following example makes clear.

Example

Investigation-based instruction and multiple means of expression open doors for students with disabilities[24]

When the suburban Mid-Atlantic district where Tess Edinger teaches shifted from a traditional science curriculum to instruction centered on exploration and investigation, "that was a big door opener" she says—particularly for the children with disabilities that she works with.

---

[24] Based on interview with Tess Edinger.

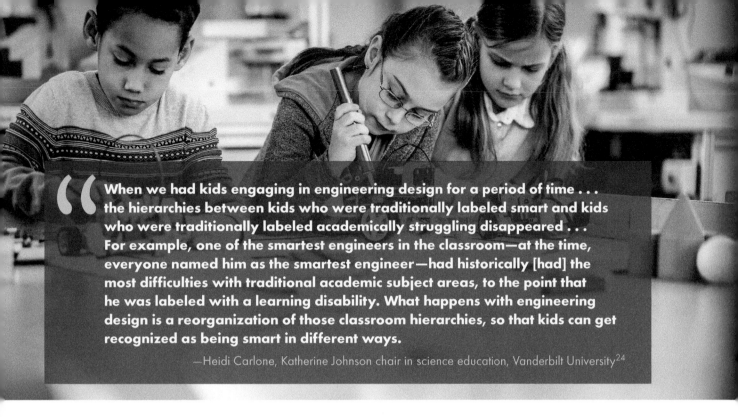

> "When we had kids engaging in engineering design for a period of time . . . the hierarchies between kids who were traditionally labeled smart and kids who were traditionally labeled academically struggling disappeared . . . For example, one of the smartest engineers in the classroom—at the time, everyone named him as the smartest engineer—had historically [had] the most difficulties with traditional academic subject areas, to the point that he was labeled with a learning disability. What happens with engineering design is a reorganization of those classroom hierarchies, so that kids can get recognized as being smart in different ways.
>
> —Heidi Carlone, Katherine Johnson chair in science education, Vanderbilt University[24]

Special educators are always looking for multiple means of engagement, expression and representation. The focus on asking questions, investigating, modeling, and collecting data "has been really powerful for our students, and given everybody equal access to things," Ms. Edinger explains. "Every student can ask a question—they may ask it using the device, they may ask it at a much more basic level—but every student can engage in that practice of asking questions." Similarly, the emphasis on making models "aligns perfectly" with the communication needs of her students "because we can use visual models, we can use tangible models, we can use computer-based models."

This flexibility extends to how students make observations and record data, notes Ms. Edinger:

> My student who has a physical impairment might be recording data on their tablet, their assistive technology, where they're using their visual picture system to make observations of what it looks like. Whereas my student who has dyslexia might not be writing, but they might be recording into their computer all of their observations verbally while they're engaging in that experiment. And then I might have a third student who's writing, so that's multiple means of expression.

For example, in one fifth-grade science unit, students make terrariums that represent all four elements of the earth's systems (geosphere, biosphere, hydrosphere, and atmosphere). Then they observe their terrariums over time to see how the systems interact. When a teacher asked

---

[25] Interview, Jan. 31, 2022.

students to write a paragraph in their science notebooks about their observations of what each component of the terrarium represents in terms of the Earth's systems and how they interact, Ms. Edinger asked the teacher whether students could meet this goal in another way. One of Ms. Edinger's students who had difficulties with fine motor skills used an iPad and a stylus to draw a diagram of his terrarium with arrows and labels to show the different components of the system. He took a picture of the screen, and Ms. Edinger printed it out so he could put it in his journal.

In a first-grade unit on sound, students go on "sound walks" inside and outside the school, where they listen for different sounds and look for the things that created those sounds. They record their observations in their notebooks. Then they share and discuss their observations. For this activity, a student in a wheelchair "can go and listen to different sounds, and they take their journal, and record things. For my students who might have some fine motor impairments, we might be taking pictures of things that they hear that make sound and annotate." Ms. Edinger's students also use various means to share their observations:

> If they took a picture of it, they would be invited up in front of the class to show the picture that they took, or if they took a little quick video of something, to show the video that they took, projected on the screen.

Ms. Edinger's biggest challenge is to help classroom teachers shift their mindset to understand that content can be expressed in multiple ways:

> The conversation that I've had most often with teachers is, yes, [my students] can do this. And they don't need to write about it to tell you that they know that this sound made this noise or that this part of their terrarium represents this system of Earth. And that's part of why we've done, as a county, a lot of PD for all of our teachers on science journals and how to use them, because we really want that journal to be a very open and flexible format for students to be representing what they know.

Let children use their own words

In oral communication, children express ideas using their own words, including everyday language, coined words, or words in a language other than English. By listening for the intent behind these words, you can guide them toward understanding a science or engineering disciplinary core idea. Consider these examples:

- **Onomatopoeic words.** In a third-grade lesson, a group of multilingual learners plucked a stringed instrument to investigate the relationship between properties like the length of a string and the sound it makes. The children described the higher-pitched sound made by the shortest string as "ting ting" and the lower-pitched sound as "tong tong." John Dahl, the teacher, realized that these sound associations could help students make a connection between the length of the string and its pitch. A child named Mei proposed that the sound difference occurred "because of the size. Because when you put the ruler longer, it make, like, 'tooooong' . . . And when you put the ruler shorter, it makes 'tiiiiing.'"[26]

- **Everyday words.** During a cold New England winter, a fourth-grade teacher picked up on a student's comment that "sweaters are hot" to teach her class about sources of heat. Many students seemed to believe that the clothing itself generated heat. "If you put a thermometer inside a hat, would it ever get hot!" said one student. The children tested this idea multiple times and were baffled when thermometers placed inside sweaters, hats, and sleeping bags on a table did not show a temperature rise. The difference between emitting heat and holding heat seemed to be eluding them. Rather than directly teaching her student about thermal insulation, she asked them if they could think of anything that "trapped" heat, that kept things warm without heating them. While some students clung to their theory that the heat was coming from the sweater, several began to understand that the heat that seems to come from "warm" clothes actually emanates from their warm bodies and is trapped inside the clothes.[27]

Be attentive to the communication needs of multilingual learners.

Allowing and even encouraging multilingual learners to use words in their first language can help them learn science and engineering content more effectively. When children use their first language, they can focus on the science. For example, in a fifth-grade science class with many emergent multilingual learners and a bilingual teacher, children move flexibly between Spanish and English in speaking, writing, and creating digital images. This flexibility helps them learn technical vocabulary, use visual supports to extract information from texts, and categorize objects by similar characteristics.[28]

---

[26] Suárez, E., & Otero, V. (2023). Ting, tang, tong: Emergent bilingual students investigating and constructing evidence-based explanations about sound production. *Journal of Research in Science Teaching.* https://doi.org/10.1002/tea.21868

[27] Watson, B., & Konicek, R. (1990). Teaching for conceptual change: Confronting children's experience. *Phi Delta Kappan* (May), 680–685.

[28] Poza, L. E. (2016). The language of ciencia: Translanguaging and learning in a bilingual science classroom. *International Journal of Bilingual Education and Bilingualism, 21*(1), 1–19.

If you don't know the language being spoken by a child or many children, it's still okay to let them speak in their first language. Even though you may not always know what they're saying, other students who speak that language can converse with them about science ideas, and some may be able to translate. If you are able to learn a few key words in a language spoken by children in your class, this will forge a connection.[29]

Productively introduce scientific vocabulary in context

To participate fully in scientific and engineering discourse, students at some point will need to learn key vocabulary of these disciplines. However, the traditional approach of first teaching children the science or engineering terms for the underlying concepts you want them to learn is ineffective for developing either their language skills or their understanding of key concepts.

Imagine a teacher who introduces the day's learning goals by writing on the board, *We will understand and explain thermal equilibrium.* The teacher asks the children to repeat the term "thermal equilibrium" in unison and then gives them a definition before launching into an investigation to demonstrate the concept. Contrast this with a teacher who tells the class that today "we will investigate what happens when we put a container of hot water into a container of cold water." Only after the children have conducted this investigation does the class jointly construct language to describe the phenomenon they observed.

The second teacher is using the research-validated approach of letting children discover concepts first and then introducing important science or engineering vocabulary in context—summed up by the phrase "activities before concepts, concepts before vocabulary." This approach emphasizes what children understand rather than whether they are using appropriate vocabulary. The vocabulary will come.

You can listen for key moments during children's conversations and use them as a bridge to introduce a scientific term. Here's an example:

Ms. Quinn,[30] the first-grade teacher introduced at the beginning of this chapter, values "kid talk" but also wants the children to learn scientific terminology once they have some conceptual grounding. In an initial lesson on magnets, she notices that the students use the term "stick" to describe what happens when a magnet gets close to certain objects. Toward the end of that lesson, Ms. Quinn announces, "I am going to teach you the science word for *stick.* When they go together, we call that *attract.*" From

---

[29] Science 20/20. (n.d.). *A case of setting science talk norms.* https://www.science2020k-5.com/_files/ugd/cb74d3_f2eec51bcc9e4a0bbc7e2c49bde83b56.pdf

[30] Bismack & Haefner, 2020.

this point, Ms. Quinn generally uses the scientific term with the children. She gently reintroduces the term "attract," while making clear that she understands what children mean when they say "stick." Her primary focus is on what children understand rather than on whether they use the correct vocabulary.

As children begin to communicate using more science and engineering vocabulary, often children may productively mix or use close approximations. In Mr. Dahl's classroom, where students used onomatopoeic sounds to describe pitch, the children occasionally tried to use scientific language, as in this example:[31]

Ollie: [The shortest string] goes ting ting because it hibernates faster.

Mei: Hibernates?

Ollie: Vibernates! . . . because the smaller ruler made a high pitch noise.

Eventually, the students realize that the child means "vibrate," a word that has come up in a previous discussion. The teacher allows this exchange to play out to give students a chance to make the link between their first-hand experience and scientific language.

You can also guide the class in co-constructing definitions of key terms. This may require some up-front planning to identify a child-friendly version of the definition you eventually want them to grasp. As students come to understand more, you can work with them to collectively refine the initial definition. To do this, it is important to trust your students and be patient as they construct their understanding.

Give students time to think before responding

Extending the time you give students to process and think before answering a question is a simple but effective way to encourage equitable participation and elicit better responses in classroom discussion. Many children may need time to organize their ideas or find the words. Emergent multilingual learners may need time to translate a question in their minds.

Think-pair-share is a specific approach that gives all children time to think before they join in a whole-class conversation. The teacher poses a question and asks students to silently think about their answer for about 30 seconds, and then briefly talk to a peer to compare their responses. Then the students return to the whole-class conversation to share their ideas.

---

[31] Suarez & Otero, 2023.

Connect to children's real-life experiences

Drawing on children's experiences in discussions and investigations can encourage participation by all children, particularly those who might typically hang back or be left out. You can connect children's home, family, and cultural experiences with science and engineering disciplinary core ideas to broaden everyone's views of "what counts" as science and inspire them to think in new ways. Laura Harmon, a second-grade teacher whose class includes many emergent multilingual learners, uses various techniques to connect classroom discussion and investigations with her students' real lives:[32]

During a science unit on soil, Ms. Harmon connects her students with their local environment by having them dig soil samples and collect data from three diverse habitats within walking distance of their school. After the children do additional research on soil, Ms. Harmon asks them to take home what they have learned and interview their parents. Following these interviews, Kebba reports that in his native Gambia, "the soil is red and dusty, some places have good soft clay and are good for farming." Ying's grandmother, who is Hmong, visits the class and speaks through an interpreter. She compares the rich soil of rainy Laos with the loose, sandy soil of the U.S. Midwest and tells the children that she was "so surprised to see corn growing in rows in the sandy soil." Enriched by these experiences, the children undertake another investigation in which they try to identify unlabeled samples of soil taken from their outdoor digs. Kebba, who has become intrigued with different colors and textures of soils, quickly identifies the wet, dark black soil sample as coming from the marsh environment.

Consider how your own ways of communicating may affect students

How you talk to and work with students affects how they participate and interact in the classroom. For example, if a teacher inadvertently directs different kinds of questions to children from historically marginalized groups, this can negatively affect their desire to participate and self-identity as a doer of science and engineering. By contrast, teacher talk that is equitable and doesn't make presumptions about students can serve as a model for the children in the class.

It's a matter of practice

You may be awed by colleagues who appear to orchestrate discussions and collabora-

---

[32] Example from National Science Teaching Association. (2013). *NGSS case study 4: English Language Learners and the Next Generation Science Standards.* https://ngss.nsta.org/case-study-4.aspx

tive work like maestros. With an open mind, reflection, and practice, you can become effective in structuring student interactions that lead to learning. Jeanane Charara, a professional development provider and instructional coach for grades K–2, points out that when she first starts coaching teachers on an integrated science and literacy curriculum that emphasizes investigations, discussions, and group work, many of the teachers are "not very confident." But then,

> [O]ver time, it starts to become very natural in their structure. So maybe they started with constantly glancing at what types of questions they need to ask. Now they're at the point where, when they're meeting with students in small groups, they're naturally asking those questions.[33]

The results of seeing all your students contribute and learn is well worth the effort. You will get to see how students gain a greater sense of agency through collaborative communication, which not only has the potential to increase their investment in learning, but their pride.

QUESTIONS FOR REFLECTION

- What biases or expectations do I hold for how my students can work together?

- How can I plan for and model productive talk?

- How can I plan for and model inclusive talk that avoids presumptions based on race, ethnicity, language, and other characteristics?

- How can I become more comfortable guiding students' thinking even when their ideas are incomplete or incorrect?

- How can I encourage students to reflect on their discussion and ways of interacting?

---

[33] Interview, Dec. 7, 2021.

6

Revealing Learning through Assessments

As children carry out investigations and design tasks; as they model, write, and draw; and as they reason, discuss, argue, and engage in other activities described in the previous chapters, they are learning. They are also revealing information about how they think, what they know and don't know, and where they need more support. You can use this information to plan and adjust your instruction to better meet their needs as they progress toward learning targets—in other words, to engage in assessment.

Assessment is an integral part of instruction. You no doubt use it regularly to get feedback on learning for both individual children as well as the whole class, and then use that feedback to figure out your next instructional steps. In classrooms centered on actively engaging students in scientific investigation and engineering design, opportunities for assessment are all around you. Often, these opportunities are so closely intertwined with effective instructional strategies as to be inseparable.

This chapter is *not* about the standardized tests given at the end of a unit or school year, nor is it about grading. It is about classroom-based formative and summative assessment. This includes assessment evidence you gather through children's discussions and written work, self/peer assessment, and more formal summative assessments. This chapter discusses and gives examples of various strategies you can readily use to better understand how your students are engaging in three-dimensional learning.

What does assessment look like in a science classroom?

In a unit designed to help second graders learn how water shapes land, students make models, build small dams, and engage in other tasks. The following case shows how models and explanations can be embedded as a way to assess children's understanding of disciplinary core ideas and engagement in science practices. Notice how the teacher, Ms. Vaughan, not only analyzes children's models to assess each child's thinking, but also organizes information from the models to advance learning for the whole class.

Models and other tools reveal children's ideas about how some floods happen[1]

In 1914, the city of Seattle finished building a new dam out of stone, brick, and mortar on the Cedar River. A few months later, the people of nearby Moncton, a town on the other side of a mountain from the dam, began to notice puddles forming in their streets. One night, the water rose six inches and the wooden sidewalks started floating. By May of 1915, the water was rising a foot a day. By summer of that year, the people of Moncton had to evacuate, as the water rose to the roofs of their houses.

What does this long-ago local history have to do with science instruction? It's the entry point for a unit on water and landforms centered around this puzzling phenomenon: *What caused the town of Moncton to flood?* Annie Vaughan, a second-grade school teacher in Washington State, shares the story of Moncton with her class in the third lesson of a unit. Over the next few months, in 45-minute science lessons taught two or three times a week, the students explore that question.

After telling the story, Ms. Vaughan asks students to share their own experiences with water and flooding, including a recent time when their schoolyard and classroom flooded after a heavy rain. The children discuss their initial questions and ideas about the Moncton flood. They look at before-and-after photos of the area surrounding the town and watch a video.

Assessing initial models

Working with partners, students draw models to show their initial thinking about how and why the town flooded, using templates provided by

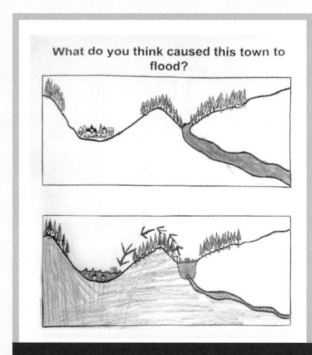

Figure 6-1. Model of a child's initial idea of what caused a town to flood. Drawings show the landscape before (top) and after (bottom) a dam was built

Source: Salgado & Salgado, 2019.

---

[1] This case was developed from Salgado, M., & Salgado, N. (2019). *NGSS stories: A second grade classroom explores the flooding of the town of Moncton* [Conference session]. La Cosecha Dual Language Conferences, Albuquerque, New Mexico; Salgado, M. & Phelps, D. (2021). *Approaches to research and design: Engaging young children in science and engineering practices* [Conference session]. NARST; Shim, S.-Y., Thompson, J., Richards, J., & Vaa, K. (2018). Agree/disagree T-charts. *Science and Children, 56*(1), 39–47; and the Ambitious Science videos on Argumentation and Modeling for the Teaching Channel. https://www.teachingchannel.com/k12-hub/blog/scientific-argumentation/

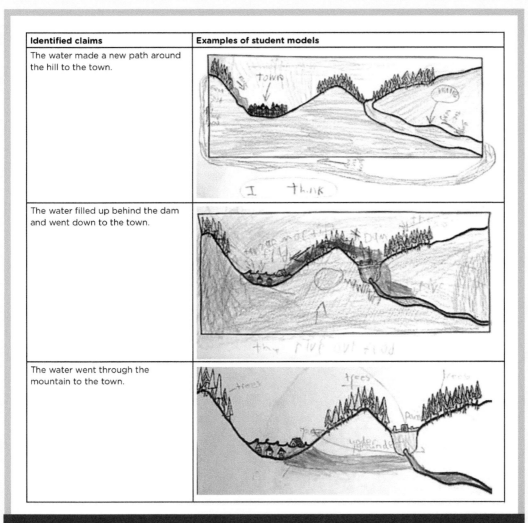

Identified claims	Examples of student models
The water made a new path around the hill to the town.	
The water filled up behind the dam and went down to the town.	
The water went through the mountain to the town.	

Figure 6-2. Claims identified from students' initial models and examples of each claim

Source: Shim et al., 2018.

the materials with preprinted outlines of the river, mountain, and town before and after the dam was built. Figure 6-1 shows an example of one child's "before-and-after" model created using the template.

After school, Ms. Vaughan examines students' models to assess their initial ideas about how water moves above and through earth. She groups their initial ideas for why the town flooded into three main categories (Figure 6-2):

- Water from the river might make a new path around the mountain.

- The dam might stop the water, causing it to overflow and move over or around the mountain into the town.

- The water could go through the earth materials in the mountain to get into the town.

The third category of responses is closest to the scientific explanation that Ms. Vaughan wants the children to eventually arrive at: the town filled up because water moves through the mountain, which was a glacial moraine consisting of loose pebbles and sand deposited when the glaciers receded. However, all the children's responses reveal some understanding of disciplinary core ideas about how land and water interact and how landforms are created or shaped. Ms. Vaughn recognizes she can use basic ideas underlying these initial claims to plan future instruction.

- The claim that water made a new path around the hill to the town invites children to consider the processes of erosion and the conditions that promote it or slow it down.

- The claim that water filled up behind the dam can encourage students to ask questions and analyze data about how much rain fell in the flood year and whether the dam filled up more quickly than it released water.

- The claim that water went through the mountain connects to disciplinary core ideas about the properties of the materials that make up the Earth, permeability, and absorption.[2]

Figure 6-3. Children make their thinking visible by placing their ideas on an agree/disagree chart

Source: Shim et al., 2018.

By grouping children's models in this way, Ms. Vaughan can see the different kinds of understanding that children bring to the unit. She uses this information to structure further discussion and investigation to support children as they develop their understanding and refine their explanatory models.

Gaining additional insights from discussion

To support children in generating and refining claims, assembling evidence, and developing arguments and consensus models, Ms. Vaughan uses an "agree/disagree t-chart," a tool she helped to develop. By making children's reasoning visible, this tool also serves as a form of assessment.

To spark discussion, Ms. Vaughan makes three t-charts, one for each of the three main claims described above (Figure 6-3). She initially places students' models beside the claim that she thinks they go with, then invites students to tell her if they

---

[2] Shim et al., 2018.

agree with this placement. Some children move their models, while others ask to put their models on more than one claim.

Next, Ms. Vaughan invites children to write or draw on a sticky note about a past experience they had with water movement or flooding and to share these ideas with the class. These might range from building a dam at the beach to playing with water in the bathtub. For example, one child describes how she and a friend pushed water off the concrete surface of the playground into the dirt, where it immediately soaked into the ground instead of puddling. This sharing leads to a class discussion of whether the personal experiences agree (support) or disagree with (refute) the three claims and where to put them on the t-charts. This discussion and the charts encourage children to articulate their reasoning and identify supporting evidence, while giving Ms. Vaughan more information about how students' thinking is evolving and how to connect instruction to their everyday lives.

Over several weeks, Ms. Vaughan's students amass more evidence on the structure and properties of matter to help answer the question of what caused the flood. Working in small groups, they develop and use models of landscapes out of pebbles, sand, and soil and observe how water flows through them. They design and build small dams to see how dams change the flow of water, and do other investigations and readings. With scaffolding by Ms. Vaughan, children seek to make sense of this evidence by looking for patterns and use it to engage in argument from evidence and develop final models.

Assessing final models and explanations

Near the end of the unit, for summative assessment purposes, Ms. Vaughn closely compares her students' final models and written explanations with their initial models. She's particularly interested in discerning how much children's explanations for the flooding have deepened as a result of their collaborative work and how they have used evidence to refine their models and explanations. To help her with this summative assessment, she employs a rubric, described later in this chapter. To assess how well children used evidence, Ms. Vaughan looks at how they connected data from multiple sources (investigations, personal experience, texts, video, etc.) to support their explanations.

Based on this assessment, Ms. Vaughan finds that most of the children understand that water from the dam went through the mountain or around the mountain to the town. Most of the models show the water flowing through earth materials by "zooming in" on the mountain or the ground. She sees that the majority of her students described or used more than two pieces of evidence, although some did not explain how this evidence supported their explanation. In future science and engineering units, she'll continue to emphasize the importance of evidence and reasoning.

Inspiration board: Learning from the case

From the beginning to the end of the unit, Ms. Vaughan drew from multiple sources of evidence—models, personal experiences, and discussion—to inform her instruction. Several ideas from the case could be especially helpful as you work on incorporating assessment into your daily instruction.

- **Ms. Vaughan assessed for multiple purposes throughout instruction.** Near the beginning of the unit, she elicited students' understanding of and personal experiences with water to plan future instruction and scaffolding. During class activities, she listened, questioned, and observed to determine whether children could connect their models and evidence from their investigations with explanations for a phenomenon. At the end of the unit, she assessed students' final models in terms of their depth of understanding and quality of evidence use. Her review of final models served as both a summative assessment and a source of information for future investigations.

- **Embedding assessment into instruction requires planning.** Most, if not all, of Ms. Vaughan's assessment approaches were embedded in effective instructional strategies involving science and engineering practices. These included developing models, engaging in discourse, constructing explanations, and arguing for those explanations. But she still had to plan ways to draw out each child's thinking and understanding of specific disciplinary core ideas as they engaged in these practices—for example, by having children determine where their models and experiences fit on an agree/disagree chart.

- **Ms. Vaughan used a local phenomenon and elicited children's personal experiences to inform instruction.** Because the Moncton flood occurred in the local geographic area, it may interest children more than a distant event—this can serve as a pre-assessment to gauge students' initial understanding of water. By asking children to share their own experiences with water, she validated these experiences as meaningful evidence. She also used these experiences as a springboard for productive discussions of science ideas and as practice in argumentation (*I agree, I disagree*).

- **Children's initial models and claims not only provided evidence for the teacher but also served as the basis for children's learning.** The models children made near the beginning of the unit gave Ms. Vaughan insights into their developing understanding, which she used to organize their ideas into three initial claims. Throughout the unit, Ms. Vaughan linked instruction back to these initial models, and children continued to revisit and revise them as they gathered more evidence. The initial models also served as a baseline for determining how children's understanding, and their ability to express their understanding, developed and deepened over the course of the unit.

The sections that follow focus on how you can support students in making their ideas and capabilities visible for purposes of assessment and instruction, with additional examples from Ms. Vaughan's class.

What purposes can assessment serve for three-dimensional learning?

Typically, assessments focus on determining what children know and understand. This type of information about children's understanding (and misunderstanding) of disciplinary core ideas will help you plan instruction and determine what kinds of supports children need. In classrooms anchored in investigation and design, there's an additional consideration—namely, that assessment, like instruction, should address *all three dimensions* of science and engineering learning.

Therefore, when you're working with preschool and elementary children in a classroom oriented toward three-dimensional learning, assessment can help you accomplish the following purposes:

- Understand the interests and cultural and linguistic resources of children and their families.

- Determine how well children understand and can apply disciplinary core ideas and crosscutting concepts.

- See whether and how children are engaging in science and engineering practices.

- Decide on next steps for the classroom community. This might include information you can use to help children collaborate, think critically, develop explanations, or engage in argument.

- Understand students' experiences, so you can monitor and adjust classroom expectations and structures.

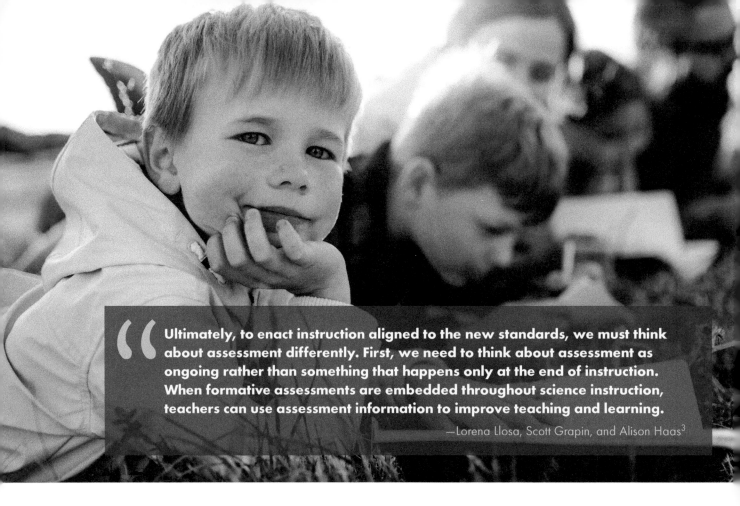

> " Ultimately, to enact instruction aligned to the new standards, we must think about assessment differently. First, we need to think about assessment as ongoing rather than something that happens only at the end of instruction. When formative assessments are embedded throughout science instruction, teachers can use assessment information to improve teaching and learning.
>
> —Lorena Llosa, Scott Grapin, and Alison Haas[3]

How can I provide supports for children to show their understanding and skills?

Just as you provide scaffolding during instruction to help children learn, you can provide specific types of supports during assessment to help children demonstrate what they know, care about, and can do. Instruction anchored in investigation and design opens up a variety of approaches, formats, and contexts for assessment. As you weigh different assessment approaches, you might keep in mind the general suggestions in Box 6-1.

Several assessment approaches have already been mentioned throughout the book. For example, as described in Chapter 5, classroom discussions often reveal what children know and wonder about. During discussions, you can use multiple forms of evidence by allowing them to record a word, phrase, or drawing on an individual whiteboard; use gestures; or answer in multiple languages if necessary. When you ask students to demonstrate their understanding through drawings, models, and other artifacts, you can also encourage them to label and talk about the artifacts, instead

---

[3] Llosa, L., Grapin, S., & Haas, A. (n.d.). *Integrating science and language for all students with a focus on English language learners: Formative assessment in the science classroom* [Brief 7]. SAIL, New York University. https://www.nysed.gov/sites/default/files/programs/bilingual-ed/brief-7-formative-assessment-in-the-science-classroom-a.pdf

of assuming the artifact alone is enough to show their thinking. In other classroom tasks, you can make sure to allow students to express their understanding in multiple ways—not only across the scope of a unit but for individual assignments.

Below are some additional examples of how you can support students in conveying their ideas as they engage in assessment tasks.

Connect to children's home and community experiences

Classroom learning activities that connect with children's home and community experiences can not only make instruction more relevant and meaningful but can also be a source of assessment information about the interests, experiences, and prior knowledge of children and families. Here are some examples that can provide important information about students' time outside of school that you can build on in your teaching:[4]

- Talk with and listen to children by facilitating "question of the day" activities that invite children to share

- Observe and listen to children as they play

- When beginning an instructional unit, provide an opportunity for students to express what they think they know and what experiences they have had related to the topic

- Directly learn what families know and do through joint activities and parent-teacher discussions

- Indirectly learn what families know and do by asking parents and children to take walks along their regular neighborhood routes and take photos to share what they notice and experience, as in Figure 6-4

- Send home brief information sheets for students to return that ask children and families to do something simple and safe involving science or engineering, such as looking for and listing examples of fruits and vegetables[5]

Provide guidance to children as they engage in a task

As children develop artifacts to document their thinking, they often need guidance about focus, structure, and expectations for content. For example, the value of notebooks as an assessment tool depends heavily on the guidance teachers give chil-

Figure 6-4. A photo of a bridge with multiple support pillars from a family's neighborhood walk and children using blocks to build the kind of bridge they saw

Source: The RISE Project.

---

[4] The RISE project, Home-School Connections, https://rise.as.tufts.edu/home-to-school/
[5] https://rise.as.tufts.edu/wp-content/uploads/2019/10/Fruits-and-Vegetables-in-My-Home.pdf

dren about what information to include in their entries.[6] However, too little or too much guidance is not helpful and limits what you are able to assess. Providing children with moderate amounts of support—such as giving them prompts while letting them draw and write what they learned in their own words—works better for both assessment and learning.

In Figure 6-5, you can see how a four-year-old first drew the seeds of a pumpkin, which are rendered as circles inside the pumpkin's outline. The child then colored over them to illustrate that the seeds are underneath the pumpkin's flesh and skin. Around the edges, you can see that a paraprofessional wrote quotes from the child's description of the drawing. In other words, the child drew what they knew, not just what they literally saw in front of them at the time, with guidance from the teacher.

Figure 6-5. A notebook drawing made by a child aged four years and 10 months

Source: Brenneman & Lauro, 2008, p. 115.

Additionally, in an upper-elementary lesson about electric circuits, some teachers gave minimal guidance to students about what to put in their science notebooks, such as "write what you learned today." The responses were often so lacking in detail that it was difficult to tell how much they understood. Other teachers were so prescriptive about format and content that the notebook entries looked as if students had just copied "right answers" from the board. A teacher named Gloria Diaz found the middle ground, offering a moderate degree of support. She provided enough structure that students knew what to focus on—in this case, comparing the brightness of a bulb in a series versus parallel circuit—so they had a good indication of what to represent in their notebooks. At the same time, students were encouraged to represent their ideas about the lesson in their own words, with symbols and/or diagrams. Their entries conveyed sufficient information for Ms. Diaz and others to monitor their understanding.[7]

Similarly, children benefit from guidance about important features to include in models and explanations. The self- and peer-assessment checklist in Figure 6-6 about elements of a landfill bottle could be used in this way. But a checklist doesn't have to be a prepared handout. Instead, you can work with students to co-develop "gotta have it" checklists for the class. This option is suggested in the materials for the water and landforms unit that Ms. Vaughan taught in the case presented earlier in

---

[6] Aschbacher, P., & Alonzo, A. (2006). Examining the utility of elementary science notebooks for formative assessment purposes. *Educational Assessment, 11*(3–4), 179–203.

[7] Aschbacher & Alonzo, 2006.

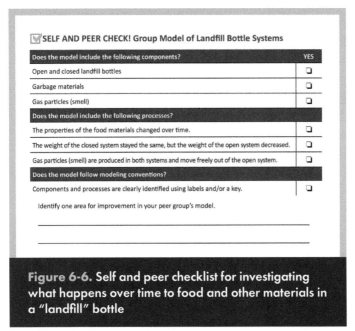

Does the model include the following components?	YES
Open and closed landfill bottles	❑
Garbage materials	❑
Gas particles (smell)	❑
Does the model include the following processes?	
The properties of the food materials changed over time.	❑
The weight of the closed system stayed the same, but the weight of the open system decreased.	❑
Gas particles (smell) are produced in both systems and move freely out of the open system.	❑
Does the model follow modeling conventions?	
Components and processes are clearly identified using labels and/or a key.	❑

Identify one area for improvement in your peer group's model.

_____

_____

Figure 6-6. Self and peer checklist for investigating what happens over time to food and other materials in a "landfill" bottle

Source: Llosa et al., n.d.

this chapter. These materials include a sample checklist with examples of elements that could be addressed in models, drawings, and explanations, such as "evidence that water can slowly and quickly change the shape of the land" and explanations of "where this particular glacial moraine comes from, what is inside [it], and why the town became flooded."[8] This sort of sample doesn't have to be taken verbatim; you could use something like this to guide students in collaboratively designing their own assessment rubrics.

Guidance could also take the form of an "anchor chart" that displays useful strategies for a particular task. An anchor chart about science observations might include such strategies as drawing what you see, focusing on what is most important, and using closeups and different views. Anchor charts can be revised or expanded as you make children's work public and discuss what kind of information helps everyone in the class know what the creator of the work is thinking.

Make resources available

A relatively simple assessment support strategy is to make resources available in the classroom where children can refer to them as needed—and to explicitly tell students why they are there. You can also point to these resources to clarify questions that come up during discussions or group work (see Chapter 5 for more on this technique). Examples include but are not limited to anchor charts, dictionaries, and lists of key terms with illustrations. To the extent possible, these resources can be provided in multiple languages to further support multilingual learners.

Probe for thinking and understanding

Previous chapters emphasized the value of asking specific questions to guide students during discussions, investigations, and other tasks. These types of probing questions

---

[8] All Circles of Learning Water Unit Guide, https://www.allciclesoflearning.com

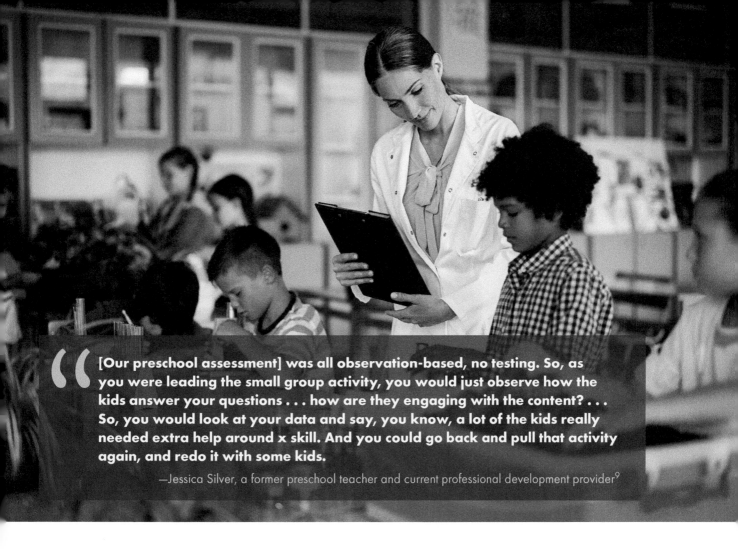

> [Our preschool assessment] was all observation-based, no testing. So, as you were leading the small group activity, you would just observe how the kids answer your questions . . . how are they engaging with the content? . . . So, you would look at your data and say, you know, a lot of the kids really needed extra help around x skill. And you could go back and pull that activity again, and redo it with some kids.
>
> —Jessica Silver, a former preschool teacher and current professional development provider[9]

also serve an assessment purpose by bringing to light information about children's thinking. Here are some examples:

- Asking children at the beginning of an investigation to make predictions and explain their rationales (Chapter 3)

- Probing children's thinking and decisions as they create models (Chapter 4) with questions like these: *What is one thing you added or changed in your final model and why? What is one piece of evidence from our evidence board that supports your model? How does your model help us explain _____?*

- Using the teacher talk moves during discussions (Chapter 5)

The following example from Ms. Vaughan's class highlights how probes can bring out children's thinking.

---

[9] Interview, May 16, 2022.

Example

Probing children's thinking in the Moncton Case

During the unit on water and landforms, students in Ms. Vaughan's class investigated how different earth materials (rocks, pebbles, sand, and soil) affected water flow by putting the different materials in funnels and pouring water on top. Students saw a pattern—water flowed more easily through earth materials with bigger particles and bigger holes between them. Ms. Vaughan now wants to see how well her students are applying ideas from their investigation to the phenomenon of the Moncton flood. She gives students the following stem of an "if-then" argument (also known as a conditional argument), along with a template to fill in: *If the glacier left mostly _____ and some _____ then . . . .* (Figure 6-7).

Throughout the different investigations in the unit, Ms. Vaughn has frequently used sentence stems like *If _____, then _____ because _____.* or *I know this because _____.* As

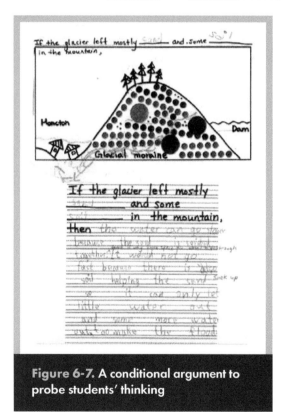

Figure 6-7. A conditional argument to probe students' thinking

Source: Shim et al., 2018.

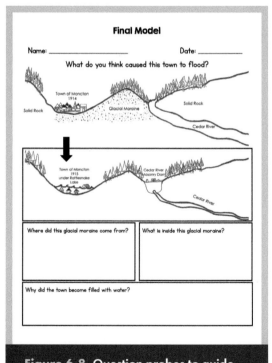

Figure 6-8. Question probes to guide children in creating a final model

Source: Salgado & Phelps, 2021.

children prepare to create their final models, Ms. Vaughan supplies them with an additional task that includes the probe *What do you think caused this town to flood?* This task is intended to further draw out their understanding of important ideas, such as these: *Where did the glacial moraine come from? What is inside the glacial moraine? Why did the town flood with water?* (Figure 6-8).[10]

How can I interpret information from assessments?

Once you've gathered assessment evidence about children's understanding and proficiency, it can still be difficult to make sense of all the information. Children's activities, talk, and work products are complex and can be interpreted through many lenses. You need to be clear about what you're looking for and aware of the biases that can affect your interpretations.

Processes for making inferences

A classroom assessment system really is a structured process for examining and interpreting children's learning over time through their classroom work. Without such a process, it's easy to get caught up in looking for textbook explanations for a phenomenon or looking at features like vocabulary, neatness, or basic writing conventions. What matters most is children's progress in developing proficiency toward specific learning goals. Therefore, a process that supports you in making inferences about children's progress and adapting your instruction accordingly should focus on these aspects:

- The learning goals for a unit of study or year of instruction;

- The resources, interests, and experiences children bring to instruction;

- The stepping stones or the knowledge, skills, and abilities needed to reach those goals; and

- The incomplete ideas that children are likely to bring and their productive ideas that you can build upon.

---

[10] Salgado, M., & Phelps, D. (2021). *Approaches to research and design: Engaging young children in science and engineering practices* [Conference session]. NARST.

From the beginning of an instructional unit, you can start thinking about what types of classroom activities and student work will yield evidence of students' progress toward designated learning goals and uncover the kinds of thinking you want to encourage.

Consider how Ms. Vaughan approached children's modeling work at the beginning of the water and landforms unit. The decisions she made were intended not only to get evidence about students' grasp of the targeted disciplinary core ideas and practices for the unit, but also to create opportunities for students to grapple with these ideas and apply these practices. In looking at children's initial models, she paid less attention to whether children "correctly" understood that the water went through the porous land. In fact, assessing for correctness at that point would likely have gotten in the way of future learning. Instead, she organized these models according to their main ideas about how water and land interact, as a way to set up future investigations that would enable students to build on those ideas over time. She asked the children themselves what experiences they had had that supported or challenged these ideas. Doing so served a dual purpose: Ms. Vaughan obtained more information about student thinking and personal contexts for learning, while the children had a chance to organize their thinking and use evidence to support and refute claims.

In general, rubrics are a vital tool to help you make inferences about children's learning. You can structure rubrics so they specify criteria for assessing students' work along a continuum of increasing proficiency in disciplinary core ideas, science practices, or both. Once again, an example comes from Ms. Vaughan's instruction.

Example

Using rubrics in the Moncton case

To assess her students' final models, Ms. Vaughan employs a rubric that describes the characteristics of explanations at different levels of proficiency: beginning, approaching, meeting, and exceeding. Table 6-1 shows the criteria for evaluating the depth of the explanation for the flood phenomenon in children's models. For example, an explanation that is "approaching" proficiency in its depth of explanation would make claims about, but neglect to explain, how or why the town flooded, as in this example: *Water went through the mountain from the dam to the town.*

TABLE 6-1

RUBRIC FOR EVALUATING MODELS IN WATER AND LANDFORMS UNIT

Level	Depth of explanation	Example of drawn, written, or verbal explanation
Beginning	Describes the observable phenomenon of the town flooding of the town	First, large puddles formed. Then the water got higher and flooded the town.
Approaching	Makes claims about how or why the town flooded	Water went through the mountain from the dam to the town.
Meeting	Explains mechanisms for how and why the construction of the dam caused the town to flood	Incorporates at least two of the following disciplinary core ideas at play in the Moncton scenario: 1) how a dam can change the flow of a river; 2) the composition of the glacial moraine in the mountain; 3) how the structure and properties of matter affect water flow; and 4) how water can change the shape of land quickly or slowly.
Exceeding	Constructs an explanation that specifies conditions under which the claims hold true	If the glacier left mostly pebbles and some sand in the mountain, then _____.

Source: All Circles of Learning Water Unit Guide.

Note how the criteria for evaluating the depth of children's explanations are based on their understanding of the specific mechanisms and ideas at play in the Moncton scenario. The criteria consider children's ability to explain what happened, attend to how it happened, and identify the specific mechanisms for why it happened. The criteria are also connected to the big ideas that students explored in the unit, such as the movement of water through land, the permeability of landforms, and the role of man-made features like dams in changing land, among others. These types of criteria allow the teacher to make inferences about how an individual student is progressing toward a learning goal, but they should not be used to make comparisons between students.

How can I assess in ways that are fair and unbiased?

Assessment, like other aspects of instruction, is most effective when all children have fair and multiple means of demonstrating what they know and can do. Equitable and relevant assessment presumes that children bring important knowledge, interests, and experience from their daily lives, which you can elicit and use to inform instruction.[11]

Some assessment tools or tasks may not accurately reveal the full range of understanding and proficiency for all children, including those from historically marginalized groups, because the tools were constructed for more homogenous groups of children. For example, if a child doesn't remember the meaning of the word "plate" when used in the geologic sense, they may not do well on an assessment question or task that includes the word "plate" in a question about how mountains are formed. The child may be thinking of a dinner plate but may nevertheless understand in some way that pieces of the earth move and collide.

In addition, when some teachers interpret information from assessments, they may judge the skills of some children differently from others based on irrelevant characteristics such as gender, race, ethnicity, disability, or English language proficiency. This, in turn, may influence how teachers facilitate and modify instruction for children.

The potential for bias in conducting and interpreting assessments is real, and reducing it requires self-monitoring and proactive steps. Many of the suggestions in earlier chapters for making instruction equitable and culturally and linguistically relevant also apply to assessment. When you're implementing and interpreting evidence from assessments, you can address potential bias with strategies like these:

- Consider data from multiple sources and from different contexts.

- Solicit input from families and other educators with expertise in working with groups of children that you might be less knowledgeable about.

- Provide multiple means for children to engage in science practices and learning activities and to express what they know, are interested in, and can do.

[11] Bell, P., Neill, T., Stromholt, S., & Shaw, S. (2018). *Making science instruction compelling for all students: Using cultural formative assessment to build on learner interest and experience* [Conference session]. https://www.oercommons.org/courseware/lesson/14482/overview

- Compare the performance of each student to the learning target, not to the performance of other students.

An example from a semi-urban school in the Northeastern U.S. highlights strategies used by Jesse Greene, an early-career kindergarten teacher, to engage and assess his students equitably in an investigation of what worms need to survive. Many of the children are from immigrant families, and many are emergent multilingual leaners. Mr. Greene, who is bilingual in English and Spanish, has thought a lot about how to effectively assess multilingual learners.

Example

Unearthing children's ideas while they worm-watch[12]

After Mr. Greene's kindergartners have finished investigating plants grown in their classroom and have figured out what plants need to survive, he spills soil from the plant pots onto the table. And look—there are worms!

Strategy: Invite children to communicate in their home language and in multiple modes. The children draw their observations of the worms and talk about what they notice and wonder. They can share in any language, or with gestures and pictures. While holding a worm in his hand, Mr. Greene asks, "What are some other wonderings? Que preguntas tenemos?" A student responds in Spanish and English that worms use their bellies to run fast.

One question posed by the children—*Do worms like water?*—strikes Mr. Greene as a promising pathway to teaching about what worms need to survive and how worms change their environment. During center time, Mr. Greene puts three trays, along with soil and water, on a table and asks a small group of students what he should do next. The children discuss as a group. Sofia suggests they put soil in only one tray.

---

[12] Brown, M., Zembal-Saul, C. & Lee, M. (2022). Formative assessment case and tools for kindergarten worm unit. *Science 20/20: Bringing language learners into focus through school–university–community partnership.* Centre for Educational Research and Innovation.

Strategy: Make space for all children to share their thinking. Give credence to voices that agree and disagree. Mr. Greene asks if anyone agrees or disagrees. Most agree, but one child, Gabe, disagrees. Gabe thinks they should put soil in all the trays since "the worms [are] not going to be on those [other] trays."

Strategy: Ask children to share their thinking and value their responses. Mr. Greene probes Gabe's thinking further: "Why won't worms be on the other trays?" Gabe explains that it's because there isn't soil in them. Again, Mr. Greene asks why Gabe thinks this. Gabe replies, "Because the dirt makes them safe." After further questioning, Gabe adds that it's because "they don't want to be wet." Mr. Greene summarizes what he calls Gabe's "prediction"—that there won't be worms in the trays with water.

Strategy: Treat alternate ideas equitably and give children a voice in decisions. Mr. Greene says the group will do an investigation that tests both ways—one test with soil in all three trays, and another with soil in just one tray. The children then decide to put a lot of water in one tray, put a little water in another, and no water in the third (the tray with soil in the second test).

As the children observe a tray containing a little water and soil, a worm moves away from the water into the soil. "Let's watch," says Mr. Greene. "Whoa! Look! Whoa!"—the worms are moving into the soil.

Strategy: Ask children to clarify when you don't understand how they phrase something. Gabe watches the moving worms and exclaims, "They found the secret place!" Mr. Greene asks, "What secret place? Where?" Gabe responds, "Behind the dirt." Mr. Greene asks, "Why?" Other students also see worms going into "the secret place."

Strategy: Make space for students to gesture and describe their gestures with words. Mr. Greene focuses the children's attention on the worms' movements and asks how the worms move. "Do they have legs and run like us?" Bibi moves her hand across the table to imitate a worm wriggling. Pointing to the gesture, Mr. Greene asks, "How would you describe that? ¿Cómo describirías eso?" and makes the same movement. Bibi replies, "They run like this" and repeats the hand movement across the table. "So they slide?" asks Mr. Green. Bibi nods yes.

As the investigations continue, Mr. Greene guides students in both written and verbal English and Spanish and listens as they figure out what the worms need to survive. He repeats the lesson with other small groups of students, allowing each group to design tests in their own way.

As the examples in this chapter illustrate, effective assessment is flexible. It takes advantage of both planned and impromptu opportunities to glean more about students' thinking and practices. Effective assessment not only reveals learning but advances it.

If you incorporate investigation and design in your instruction to some extent, even if you're not doing it as much as you'd like yet, you're already engaging children in activities and practices that yield rich evidence for assessment. The key is to be more intentional when you're designing classroom activities and guiding students' discussions and work products, so you're thinking from the outset about their assessment value and learning value.

QUESTIONS FOR REFLECTION

- How can I build in equitable opportunities to assess all children's understanding as they discuss, investigate, make models, and engage in other science practices?

- How can I plan for and welcome multiple ways for children to demonstrate what they know and can do? How do the opportunities connect to the family and community experiences?

- What guidance, materials, and other types of support can I provide to help children demonstrate their understanding and proficiency?

- What potential biases do I have and how can I reduce them when assessing and interpreting evidence from assessment?

- If I am working to expand "what counts" as science or engineering in my classroom, how can I be sure my forms of assessment align with those more expanded perspectives? For example, are children's multiple ways of knowing accepted and valued in my rubrics?

Everything Is Connected: Integrating Science and Engineering with Instruction in Other Subjects

When children learn science and engineering, they apply knowledge and skills from other subjects, regardless of whether the teacher explicitly calls attention to it. Children use language and literacy skills to write an explanation, label parts of a model, or argue based on evidence during a discussion. They employ mathematics to measure and compare quantities and graph data. They connect to social studies when they consider how an engineering design could affect potential users. They use computational thinking when they program the behavior of animals in a computer simulation. As they work in groups and follow classroom expectations, they also develop and draw on their social-emotional skills. In short, children's minds and experiences are not compartmentalized by subject matter, like elementary school schedules often are.

You may already be explicitly integrating instruction in science and engineering instruction with the teaching of ELA or mathematics, social studies, computational thinking, or social-emotional learning. Effective integration involves more than making superficial connections between subjects or tacking on an incidental task from another content area. It goes beyond having students read books or passages about science topics during circle time or creating graphs during science investigations. Effective integration leverages the connections between subjects to energize learning in both areas while also attending to children's learning in each subject. It's a way

to bring to life one of the defining features of instruction based on investigation and design—connecting learning across content areas and contexts. When done well, an integrated approach in any one subject has been shown to actually improve learning in each of the subjects being taught.

This chapter focuses on approaches that integrate science and engineering with ELA and mathematics because these latter two subjects often receive the most instructional emphasis and time in preschool and elementary classrooms. To inform and inspire you, the chapter also includes examples of teachers who are implementing this kind of integration.

What does effective integration look like?

In a Title I K–5 school in a rural Midwestern district, a third-grade teacher, Chandra Bose, incorporates components of ELA to advance students' learning during a unit that couples science investigation and engineering design. The unit is intended to help children understand the effects of different forces on the motion of objects and is centered on the driving question, *How can we design fun moving toys that other kids can build?* Throughout the unit, students make and test prototypes of moving toys, including the balloon rocket in the case below, and use them to investigate patterns of motion and the impact of forces like friction. Ms. Bose leads interactive read-alouds from pertinent fiction and nonfiction children's books.

As you go through this case, note how Ms. Bose does more than just read the books. She alternates between text readings and hands-on tasks to build students' knowledge and keep them motivated. She focuses on particular text passages to stimulate productive discussion and asks children to go back to a story to help them develop explanations *after* they have tested ways to make a balloon rocket move.

GET SET, DESIGN!

Pairing tasks and texts to learn how toys move[1]

Seated in a circle at the front of the classroom, Chandra Bose's third graders are examining three different kinds of water squirters, including a Super Soaker. This is the prelude to a set of lessons that feature the story of Lonnie Johnson, a talented Black inventor and aerospace engineer who designed the Super Soaker water squirter, to engage children in engineering design.

Observing, predicting, and testing

As the children observe the parts of the three water squirters, Ms. Bose asks them what they notice and records their responses on chart paper. A student named Raven says that one squirter looks like "an upside-down plunger." Another student, Wyatt, describes how a different squirters works: "You have to get water and then fill it up and then it's like a pump." His classmate Levi is unsure whether that squirter is really like a pump because he contends that "if you pump that, air will not come out." Ms. Bose lets Levi try out the squirter, and he concludes that "when you pull the yellow part and you put it back in, it goes back and forth and air comes out of it."

Next, Ms. Bose asks the children to predict which of the three squirters will shoot water the

farthest and to explain their reasoning. Most vote for the squirter with the longest tube. Ms. Bose asks why they think this. Two children call attention to a sticker on the toy that says it will shoot over 40 feet. A girl named Sage gives a different reason: "Because that's the longest one, and if it's longer it might absorb more water." The children plan an investigation and go outdoors to test which squirter shoots the farthest.

Connecting text readings with children's experiences, engineering ideas, and reading strategies

During the next two class sessions, Ms. Bose leads interactive read-alouds of two books about Lonnie Johnson. The first, *From Water Squirter to Super Soaker*, describes Dr. Johnson's transition from a child in Alabama who liked to figure things out to a NASA engineer, and eventually to

---

[1] This example is drawn from Fitzgerald, M. S. (2018). *Texts and tasks in elementary project-based science* [Unpublished doctoral dissertation]. University of Michigan, Ann Arbor, MI. Additional information comes from the Multiple Literacies in Project-Based Learning curriculum, third-grade unit 3.2, Toys, https://mlpbl.open3d.science/curriculum/3; and from Palincsar, A. S., Fitzgerald, M. S., DellaVecchia, G. P., & Easley, K. M. (2020). *The Integration of literacy, science, and engineering in prekindergarten through fifth grade.* The National Academies Press.

the designer of a water toy that got people really wet! The other book, *Whoosh!*, explains how Dr. Johnson designed and tested a prototype of the Super Soaker.

To prime children for the readings, Ms. Bose prompts them to recap what they learned from their earlier observations and explorations. As she reads the books aloud, she pauses periodically to ask children questions, connect the texts with their own experiences, and consider reading strategies and language. Here are a few excerpts from the interactive discussions:

Connecting with children's experiences:

Ms. Bose: What was a system or what was something that [Lonnie Johnson] found interesting that he kind of used with his robot? He used it with his robot to get his robot to move.

Raven: Force.

Effie: Compressed air.

Ms. Bose: Compressed air. Think about what we did on Friday. Do you think we were using any compressed air on Friday?

Wyatt: Yeah, loads of it.

Using descriptive words:

Ms. Bose: Just based on what we've read, what you've listened to, what kind of a person do you think Lonnie Johnson is? . . . What words would you use to describe him? Wyatt?

Wyatt: A very creative person.

Ms. Bose: Okay, so, creative. What else would you say about Lonnie Johnson? Raven?

Raven: Inventor.

Ms. Bose: Inventor *(recording student ideas on board)* . . . Aaron?

Aaron: An engineer.

Figure 7-1. Balloon rocket set-up used in classroom investigation

Photograph by Dean Johnson. https://creativecommons.org/licenses/by-nc/2.0/

Other children: Unique . . . Someone that fixes . . . A handyman.

(Part of discussion deleted)

Ms. Bose: (Reading aloud) "Science fairs came and went . . . and then another." So, I'm already thinking, what's one character trait that you could say about him?

Ty: Hardworking

Aaron: Determined

Using reading to inform an investigation

In a later lesson in the unit, Ms. Bose reads aloud a story about two children who try to build a balloon rocket but have trouble making it work. The story is designed to introduce ideas about friction and motion. After discussing the story, Ms. Bose's students plan and test various approaches for making their own balloon rocket move (Figure 7-1).

After children have finished testing their balloon rocket, they decide that it didn't move very far or fast. Ms. Bose asks children what they might do to change that. Effie points out that the balloon rocket in the story "just bounced up and down, and this one [the class rocket] did too!" Ms. Bose asks her students to go back to the story and think about what the children in the story might have done wrong, based on the class's first-hand balloon rocket tests, and whether any ideas from the story could help to explain what they found during their own investigation.

Priscilla speculates that the balloon in the story might have had a knot in its string, or the character in the story didn't tie it. Raven suggests that tying the balloon with yarn instead of twine would allow the rocket to go farther because "there wasn't as much friction" on the string. Priscilla then suggests using a thinner string "because this [the balloon rocket] gets stuck, [the twine] gets very big knots." After a question from Ms. Bose, Priscilla adds that "we should try a thinner string and then it can go [all the way up to the top], and then it doesn't stop."

Inspiration board: Learning from the case

- **Ms. Bose used the readings in a way that drew on students' thinking.** She often paused during the read-alouds to ask questions and elicit students' predictions and ideas. She linked the readings to students' own lives. The text played a critical supporting role in investigation and design work. In other words, Ms. Bose did not directly teach or tell students core science ideas from the text, but rather highlighted parts of the book that would help students arrive at the disciplinary core ideas themselves.

- **The integration of ELA with science and engineering was done in a mutually supportive way.** Rather than pulling children out of science for language support, they had opportunities to develop reading and language skills in a meaningful context. The texts and the tasks reinforced each other. For example, Ms. Bose gave students opportunities during and after the reading to brainstorm about important aspects of the engineering process and reflect on their own prototypes and testing. Asking students to identify Lonnie Johnson's character traits supported ELA goals while reinforcing a critical aspect of the engineering design process.

- **The teacher primed students ahead of time so they would get more out of the readings.** For example, she had them examine and test three water squirters before getting into the Lonnie Johnson readings. This approach let students develop some background knowledge on their own before approaching complex text.

- **The focus on a Black engineer reinforces that people who do science and engineering come from many different backgrounds.** In addition, Dr. Johnson's character traits and the many patents he holds can inspire children and strengthen their self-image. Including such texts also can support an equity move of enhancing representation, which can then help children "see themselves" as people who do science or engineering.

- **Ms. Bose included strategies for reading, vocabulary, and other ELA components in the reading portions of the lesson.** For example, she encouraged children to use evidence from the texts to support or expand on their ideas. During the readings, she sometimes explained or introduced vocabulary and asked students to come up with descriptive words. She asked children to reflect on what they read to understand character traits.

How does integration of multiple subjects benefit teachers and students?

Subject integration makes science and engineering instruction more authentic by mirroring how real scientists and engineers apply knowledge from other fields to their work. Effective integration also benefits teachers and students in other ways.

Subject integration builds on the strengths of preschool and elementary teachers

As a preschool or elementary teacher, especially in a self-contained classroom, you are likely responsible for children's development and learning in all subjects. In the early years of schooling, teaching children to read, write, speak, and listen, and to do mathematics, are typically the main focus of your job. You clearly have expertise in these subjects—and that's an asset for integrated instruction.

You probably already do some forms of integration, whether you label it that way or not. Children's trains of thought don't always fall into neat categories, and you sometimes need to address questions as they arise. For example, while reading the story of the three little pigs during an ELA block, a student might ask a question about the differences between brick, straw, and sticks—the materials the pigs used to construct their homes, with varying results. This question presents an opportunity for you to guide children to explore disciplinary core ideas related to properties of matter and the crosscutting concept of structure and its relationship to function as they reflect on why a brick house might stay standing longer than a stick house.

Subject integration can help address the problem of limited instructional time

You're well aware of the importance of teaching reading and mathematics in the early years of education and the pressure teachers often feel to raise student achievement in these subjects. With the majority of instructional time in elementary schools devoted to ELA and mathematics, the time available for science and engineering at this level is meager, on average, and even less in preschool.

Carefully integrating instruction in ELA or mathematics with science and engineering can help address this time crunch—not by making indiscriminate cuts in ELA and mathematics time but by designing ways to use class time more strategically and connect content areas more thoughtfully.

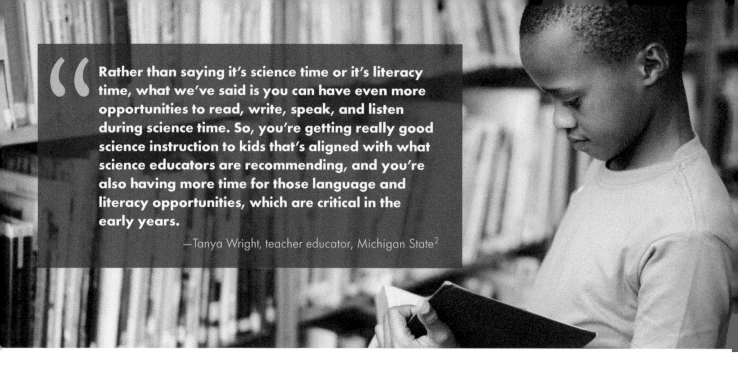

> Rather than saying it's science time or it's literacy time, what we've said is you can have even more opportunities to read, write, speak, and listen during science time. So, you're getting really good science instruction to kids that's aligned with what science educators are recommending, and you're also having more time for those language and literacy opportunities, which are critical in the early years.
>
> —Tanya Wright, teacher educator, Michigan State[2]

Subject integration can motivate and support learners with different strengths and needs

When you incorporate ELA and mathematics into science and engineering, children aren't just reading or calculating for its own sake. The goal of explaining a science phenomenon or design a solution to a problem provides a context and more compelling reason for applying ELA and mathematics practices. When children are reading, writing, or communicating about science or engineering materials and ideas that interest them, this can increase their motivation to persist through when these activities become more difficult.

Integrating other subjects with science and engineering also opens up additional ways for children to demonstrate their strengths and for you to address their needs. A fourth-grade student who struggles with some aspects of mathematics class may learn how to identify geometric shapes while designing a bridge. Marian Hobbes Moore, a STEM instructional coach, described how a "straight-backed and stern-faced" multilingual learner who seldom spoke in class found his voice while working on a project to create a solar oven:

> When we did the engineering . . . [Felipe] wasn't sure about working with other kids. So we did make sure that he was in a group where he wouldn't be intimidated. And he could actually communicate . . . He was really excited about talking about things. And he had no problem saying, Well, I think this is better because of this. And so he really came through on that in a way that I don't think anything else would have done for him.[3]

[2] Interview, Dec. 10, 2021.
[3] Interview, Feb. 12, 2022.

PRINCIPLES FOR EFFECTIVE INTEGRATION

- Engage children in investigation and design experiences that draw on multiple subjects.

- Make integration explicit when designing classroom resources and teaching strategies.

- Support children's knowledge in individual subjects.

- Recognize that more integration is not necessarily better.

What are some general principles for effective integration?

Whichever subjects you choose to connect, you may find it helpful to keep in mind the principles in Box 7-1 as you plan and implement integration.

Engage children in investigation and design experiences that draw on multiple subjects

Many domains of life intersect in real-world problems, which makes these problems a natural way to improve learning in multiple subjects. As you select phenomena for investigations and tasks for design, consider how they provide a context for or can be strengthened by knowledge and practices from other subjects. For instance, what kinds of mathematical concepts or practices might help children analyze data and notice patterns as they investigate phenomena? How can books or other texts set the stage for engineering activities or shed light on a science concept after an investigation? How can children share their findings through writing, and how can writing about science phenomena support their literacy learning?

Make integration explicit to students when designing classroom resources and teaching strategies

As you integrate activities, it's productive to identify and keep in mind your learning goals for each of the subjects involved. If a subject like mathematics is playing a supporting role, it may help you to figure out whether there's time in a lesson for children to draw on prior knowledge and skills and for you to provide scaffolding for those skills, if necessary. For example, if you have enough time, you may decide to pause a discussion of a science model to, for instance, teach children some of the mathematics behind the model. Then you can fold the science back in after children understand the mathematics. If you don't have time, you may need to quickly touch on the essential mathematics and then get back to focusing on modeling.

It can also be helpful to discuss with children the specific learning goals for each of the subjects in a lesson. If you're introducing measurement into an investigation of plant growth, for example, you could list the measurement goals (*today we're going to learn how to use a yardstick and use the units on the yardstick to measure and compare length*) as well as the science goals (*we're going to observe different patterns of plant growth and come up with explanations of things that may affect growth based on our evidence*). This kind of explicit talk about goals can help children see how mathematics and science are mutually supportive.

Find meaningful, purposeful connections to other subjects

Because every subject is unique, with its own set of knowledge and practices, different subjects present different possibilities for integration. As you design and implement integrated instruction, you should incorporate strategies that honor the knowledge and practices of each subject and support children in learning them rather than spending time on superficial connections that could interfere with the learning goals. For example, in a unit that integrates science and history, you can support children in recognizing that work in both subjects involves backing up claims with evidence, but in different ways.

Recognize that more integration is not necessarily better

Each subject area has a body of knowledge and skills that develops coherently over time. Some of these knowledge and skills may be best taught separately during time reserved for that subject. For example, you might spend several days teaching students a reading or writing skill during ELA instruction. In the process, you can alert students that this skill will come in handy for an upcoming science or engineering project. Then you can spend several days helping them apply that skill to their current science or engineering work during science time.

How can I integrate ELA with science and engineering?

Language and literacy are a means to learning any subject and are essential to learning science and engineering. Whether children are recording observations, creating models, or constructing explanations and arguments, they are using one or more of the ELA building blocks of speaking, listening, reading, and writing (or drawing).

Integrating ELA can deepen children's understanding of science and engineering while also developing their language and literacy skills. Moreover, it can cultivate competencies common to both ELA and science and engineering, such as questioning, making inferences, gleaning information from texts, and summarizing information from multiple sources.

Science and engineering can be a rich and authentic context for developing the language proficiency of all learners, and particularly for multilingual learners (see Box 7-2).

BOX 7-2

SUPPORTING MULTILINGUAL LEARNERS WITH INTEGRATED INSTRUCTION

Too often children who are multilingual learners get pulled out of science time for additional language support, often to their detriment. They not only miss out on science and engineering instruction but lose opportunities to learn language in a context that may be more motivating and showcase their strengths. Research cited in the *Brilliance and Strengths* report indicates that multilingual learners are more likely to understand and develop proficiency in English when language learning is embedded in meaningful science and engineering activities.

Ayelet Lederberg,[3] a teacher in a Midwestern city with a large immigrant population, explained how science and engineering lessons that incorporate literacy components can reinforce literacy development for her first-graders, the majority of whom are multilingual learners:

> It's not just [that] we show up for science, do an experiment, and science is a separate entity. [The students] are really getting the extra practice, which they need, in reading and writing and then applying it to real-world situations.

Many of the approaches to science and engineering education discussed in earlier chapters of this guide can benefit multilingual learners as well as all children. Examples include using stories and family connections to activate children's prior knowledge, engaging children in investigations and design tasks, and mixing up how you group students.

(Continued)

---

[4] Interview, Feb. 3, 2022.

(Continued)

In addition, you can use strategies like the following to focus specifically on the language needs of multilingual learners within an integrated approach to science and ELA instruction:[4]

- Explicitly teach key vocabulary in the context of a lesson, using English and the child's home language when possible, and provide multiple opportunities for children to use this vocabulary. You don't need to frontload vocabulary.

- Take some time to teach reading comprehension strategies when you ask children to read informational texts.

- Encourage students to record data and communicate findings in multiple modes, such as writing and speaking, gestures, and drawings, and with assistive technology.

- Use a variety of visual materials (photos, diagrams, tables, etc.) to present information and directions and help children comprehend science and engineering ideas.

- Offer various options that encourage a broad range of children to speak, such as sharing their questions, describing what they see, and explaining what they are doing.

- Vary student groupings so you sometimes group students with similar language backgrounds together and other times use heterogeneous language groups. This strategy gives students different opportunities to explain their understanding and can be especially useful for classes in which three or more home languages are represented.

Reading texts in science and engineering instruction

In traditional instruction, many teachers have relied heavily on texts to teach the science content that children are expected to learn—and remember well enough to pass a test. In instruction for three-dimensional learning, texts still play a pivotal role, but the distinction lies in *how and when* you use them.

[5] Palincsar, A. S., Fitzgerald, M. S., DellaVecchia, G. P., & Easley, K. M. (2020). *The integration of literacy, science, and engineering in prekindergarten through fifth grade.* The National Academies Press; Lee, O., Maerten-Rivera, J., Penfield, R. D., LeRoy, K., & Secada, W. G. (2008). Science achievement of English language learners in urban elementary schools: Results of a first-year professional development intervention. *Journal of Research in Science Teaching, 45*(1), 31–52; and Bravo, M. A., & Cervetti, G. N. (2014). Attending to the language and literacy needs of English learners in science. *Equity & Excellence in Education, 47*(2), 230–245.

The key is to use texts to support, rather than detract from, children figuring things out. This means using texts strategically in ways like these:

- Introduce a puzzling phenomenon or provide context for an upcoming investigation

- Present simple ideas that children will develop further when they investigate and design

- Offer another source of information to help build arguments

- Introduce or reinforce the scientific terms for concepts that children have begun to understand as a result of their previous investigations

- Connect what children are discovering to current events, related phenomena, larger ideas, or crosscutting concepts

And you're not just limited to textbooks. Various types of nonfiction and fiction texts can serve these purposes quite well. A news article like the one about the damaged shipping container on the beach in Chapter 1 can introduce a puzzling phenomenon and spur children to notice and wonder. Storybooks like the one about children sharing a bedroom in the nightlights example in Chapter 3 can set up an investigation. Text passages like those on plant parts read during the wild backyard case in Chapter 4 provide a wealth of information that children can draw on to further their understanding, make sense of their findings, and rethink their explanations. And a children's biography, like the one of Lonnie Johnson described earlier in the chapter, can provide a meaningful context while also enhancing representation (in this case) of engineers of color.

The following example shows how a teacher strategically incorporates readings from informational texts at key points during a third-grade unit on the properties of matter.

Example

Using readings to focus explorations[6]

As her class of third graders in a diverse urban school investigates solids, liquids, and gases, Rachel Meitner sometimes pauses the action to read aloud from one of several relevant children's books. She's using these texts to support, not replace, children's exploration, discussion, and discoveries.[7]

In lesson 6 of the unit, Ms. Meitner reads a passage from a children's text (*What Is the World Made of? All About Solids, Liquids, and Gases*) to help familiarize children with the properties of the three states of matter, summarized in Table 7-1.

TABLE 7-1

PROPERTIES OF STATES OF MATTER SUMMARIZED FROM A CLASS READING[8]

States of matter	Properties
Solids	Can be hard or soft Keep their shape unless you do something to them
Liquids	Have no shape, take the shape of their container Can be thick, thin, slippery, sticky Can flow or be poured
Gases	Have no shape, fill up the container they are in Most gases are invisible, but you can sometimes feel and sometimes smell them

---

[6] Example based on Varelas, M., Pappas, C. C., Kane, J. M., Arsenault, A., Hankes, J., & Cowan, B. M. (2008). Urban primary-grade children think and talk science: Curricular and instructional practices that nurture participation and argumentation. *Science Education, 92*(1), 65–95. https://doi.org/10.1002/sce.20232

[7] For teachers following the NGSS, this example is not aligned with the performance expectations for that grade level.

[8] Varelas et al., 2008, p. 72.

Ms. Meitner intentionally positions this reading before the children start a new investigation in lesson 7, but after they have developed some background knowledge and curiosity from previous lessons and a first-hand exploration of water evaporation. After the reading, the children discuss the ideas in the book. The reading and related discussion are intended to introduce a common framework—the properties scientists use to determine whether something is a solid, liquid, or gas—that can guide the students' upcoming exploration.

In lesson 7, the children are confronted with a collection of everyday objects, including liquid soap, bar soap, yarn, and a drinking straw, among others—plus several materials with "ambiguous" states of matter, such as a baggie of shaving cream, a baggie of salt, a helium balloon, a tube of paint, and a can of chicken soup. Working in small groups, the children begin their assigned task—to sort these objects into categories of solid, liquid, or gas, and then record their decisions on a data sheet. They also write explanations supporting their decisions.

As they sort, the children often disagree, argue, and change their minds. Several children refer to properties they learned from the reading to support their decisions—such as solids keeping their shape and gases having no shape—but not always in conventional or accurate ways, as these excerpts illustrate:

> **Trey:** (He takes the baggie of salt from the gases category and frowns.) Hold it.
>
> **Mateo:** What you doing?
>
> **Trey:** I'm trying to see something! (He jiggles the bag of salt.) It doesn't keep its shape. That's one point for gas. But liquid is soft.
>
> **Lin:** Ain't this [salt] a solid because look, it's like real small but it holds its shape.
>
> *(She singles out one grain of salt in the bag and looks closely at it.)*
>
> **Trey:** Who's got the salt? (Takes the baggie with the salt.) See? Look. It loses its shape.
>
> **Lin:** (Takes the baggie of salt from Trey.) Oh, but let me show you something. Look. (She takes a small grain of salt in between two fingers while it's inside the baggie.) See that little rock that just moved? . . . It still holds its shape.

Amid the disagreements, the children focus on the key properties from the previous day's reading. After the students finish classifying, recording, and explaining, they move into a whole-class discussion and produce a consensus chart.

Throughout an integrated activity, there are multiple times in which you can use texts to build on and further children's science and engineering ideas. Table 7-2 summarizes strategies you can use before, during, and after reading a text to enhance children's learning and connect it to larger concepts.

TABLE 7-2

HOW YOU CAN USE TEXTS TO BUILD ON AND FURTHER CHILDREN'S SCIENCE AND ENGINEERING IDEAS

What you can do	Examples
Before reading a text: Set a purpose for reading related to students' own work.	
Choose what part of the text you'll focus on (texts tend to have so much information that just a few pages may be enough). The disciplinary core ideas can help you make this decision	In the text about properties of matter, the teacher knew she most wanted to talk about the properties of liquids and solids, and read only a few pages around those, slowing down and focusing on the pages about properties.
Begin by discussing children's progress and naming a finding, idea, disagreement, or question that sets the stage for the text.	"I've been hearing a lot of you talking about liquids and solids lately, but we're not all sure what those words mean. Today we're going to read to see if we can find some information that will help us."
Name a particular question you want children to engage with as you're reading. Write it down so it stays visible.	"As I read, see if you can listen for how scientists tell if something is a liquid or a solid."

What you can do	Examples
During reading: Help children connect their ideas and experiences and the information in the text.	
Reinforce vocabulary to enhance the science concepts by connecting them to children's ideas rather than correcting them or asking them to repeat with "science words."	"You think that the light can't get through the cardboard? So it's an opaque material, or a material that blocks light."
Pause at important parts of the text to make sense of the information and model reading strategies.	"Maria tied the twine to a tree, pulling it as tightly as she could [*reading from the text*]. So, I'm picturing in my mind they kind of made this, right?" (*The teacher holds up the balloon rocket set up in the classroom for students to observe.*) "And she didn't just let it hang there like this. It said she did what?"[9]
Make explicit connections to children's ideas and findings.	"That reminds me of what you were saying on Monday, Destiny, about how some light was getting through the screen. So now I'm thinking that's a translucent material. It lets some light through. Do you think so too?"
After reading: Provide time and support for children to reflect on how the ideas in the text connect to their investigation and experiences.	
Go back to children's claims and evidence, explanations, or models. Ask children to think with you about how the text connects with what they have found out. Ask if there is anything else you should add to the model or explanation based on the text.	"I feel like this might help us explain why the maple seed spins the way it does. Should we look at that page again? Can anyone hear something we should add to our explanation?"

Reading suitable texts as part of science and engineering instruction can fulfill another vital purpose—to reinforce children's identities as scientists and engineers and see themselves represented in these fields. You may find the following suggestions helpful:

- **Use texts to broaden the perspective of who does and uses science and engineering.** Choose texts (and videos) that represent the identities and cultures of

---

[9] Fitzgerald, 2018, p. 189.

children in your class and the larger society, with careful attention to groups that have been marginalized in science and engineering work. In addition to the Lonnie Johnson book described in the toys case above, children can read about figures as diverse as astronaut Mae Jemison, chimpanzee expert Jane Goodall, inventor Lewis Latimer, and animal behaviorist Temple Grandin, to name just a few. And don't forget people who use science for societal goals, such as African reforestation advocate Wangari Maathai or protector of Indigenous waters Rachelle Figueroa.

- **Choose books that show children doing science and engineering.** In the *Cece Loves Science* series by Kimberly Derting and Shelli R. Johannes, for instance, Cece is constantly asking questions and developing investigations. In *Jabari Tries* by Gaia Cornwall, Jabari sets out to build a flying machine but gets frustrated when his first design doesn't work; things go better after he brainstorms ideas with his dad and little sister. These kinds of readings create opportunities for children to discuss science and engineering practices and connect them to their lives, interests, and communities.

- **Consider how science and engineering are portrayed in texts.** Not all texts are aligned with a vision of science education that is anchored in investigation and design and emphasizes equity and justice. Look for books that don't just convey facts or describe inventions, but that highlight the practices and trials that went into arriving at findings or solving problems.

In addition to reading, the ELA components of writing, drawing, and speaking can enrich science and engineering instruction when they are thoughtfully integrated. Chapters 4, 5, and 6 already include examples of how teachers have done this, and you can come up with many more creative possibilities.

How can I integrate mathematics with science and engineering instruction?

Mathematics is integral to science and engineering. When children do science and engineering, they see how useful mathematics can be in their daily lives. You can strengthen children's appreciation for and understanding of mathematics by helping them use mathematics skills and concepts to investigate phenomena and solve problems that are interesting and relevant. In turn, applying mathematics allows children to deepen their understanding of science and engineering ideas.

Chapter 4 talked about two key uses of mathematics that can be readily inte-

> **Simply by engaging students in this type of three-dimensional learning, teachers create an environment that promotes rich language use. As students develop models, analyze and interpret data, and argue from evidence with peers and their teacher, they use language to accomplish specific goals.**
>
> —Lorena Llosa, Alison Haas, Scott Grapin, and Okhee Lee[9]

grated into science and engineering lessons—measuring quantities or attributes; and organizing, interpreting, and representing data. Below are more detailed examples of how you can integrate measurement and data applications into science and engineering instruction.

Measurement in science and engineering instruction

As you incorporate measurement into science investigations and engineering tasks, there are several things to consider. The measurement experiences should strengthen children's learning in mathematics as well as science and engineering. But the mathematics shouldn't be so far beyond what children have learned that it's discouraging. You'll need to draw on your knowledge of how children develop an understanding of measurement. You may need to pause a science lesson to provide just-in-time instruction in the necessary mathematics skills and some scaffolding for children who are having difficulty.

Think of preschoolers discussing and investigating the conditions and resources that plants need to grow. To explore cause and effect, children might track growth over time as they water class plants and put them near windows to get sunlight.

---

[10] Llosa, L., Haas, A., Grapin, S., & Lee, O. (n.d.). *Integrating science and language for all students with a focus on English language learners: A classroom example* [Webinar]. https://www.nyusail.org/webinar-and-brief-5

Children may also compare the growth of different plants, or similar plants under different conditions such as plants located next to or away from a window. To conduct these investigations, children need to learn how to measure, regardless of whether they use a standard tool like a ruler or a nonstandard tool like a length of rope. They also need to figure out which measuring tools can help them observe, record, and compare changes over time. For example, is a ruler long enough to measure plants as they grow taller?

Example

Using measurement in investigations[11]

In Jonathan Fauntroy's preschool class, children want to see how much their classroom plants have grown over time. They decide to use unifix cubes to measure and compare the height of the plants. Mr. Fauntroy circulates among the children, asking questions and providing support as needed. He calls attention to one-to-one correspondence and encourages children to make comparisons, as in these excerpts from the class:

Excerpt 1:

> **Mr. Fauntroy:** Wow! How tall is your plant? (Child counts the cubes stacked in a tower next to the plant)
>
> **Mr. Fauntroy:** Great job counting—I like how you counted one by one.
>
> (After the children count how many units tall their plant is, they began to share and compare their findings with classmates.)
>
> **Owen:** Mine is 9 units tall, how many is yours?
>
> **Tia:** Mine is 11 units tall, it is the tallest.
>
> **Mr. Fauntroy:** Wow! I like how you are comparing how tall your plants are. Look at these. Which is taller—7 units or 9 units?

[11] Dominguez, X., Vidiksis, R., Leones, T., Kamdar, D., Presser, A. L., Bueno, M., & Orr, J. (2023). *Integrating science, mathematics, and engineering: Linking home and school learning for young learners.* Digital Promise, Education Development Center, GBH. https://digitalpromise.dspacedirect.org/server/api/core/bitstreams/dd63fe27-fb4f-4cdb-b40a-a2c9342de88c/content

Excerpt 2:

Mr. Fauntroy: Last time we measured our plant do you remember how tall it was?

Children: It was small.

Mr. Fauntroy: Before the weekend (checks the journal), it was this tall.

(All the children count 13 units together.)

Mr. Fauntroy: Let's measure it now. Where should I put this to start measuring? (Children point to the bottom of the measuring strip.)

Mr. Fauntroy: Amazing . . . Let's see where is it now? (Everyone counts together.) What's after fourteen?

Children: Fifteen! (See Figure 7-2)

Figure 7-2. Preschool children measure plants with unifix cubes

Source: Dominguez et al., 2023.

Data representation and analysis in science and engineering

You've probably done mathematics lessons in which children collect and graph data about their preferences, such as counting and graphing how many children in class like a specific fruit or are wearing certain clothes. In science investigations and engineering design, the data-related activities move beyond these basics and involve children looking for patterns and aggregating results across multiple cases. This allows children to deepen their understanding of both science and engineering *and* mathematics.

Recall Ms. Jafri, who first appeared in Chapter 4 as she guided her third graders through investigations of wild plants outdoors and fast-growing plants in the classroom.[12] To build on children's developing knowledge of plants and measurement, Ms. Jafri asks her students to compare plants grown in three different conditions—sun only, sun and shade, and shade only. She wants the students to use their comparative data to reach conclusions about any variations they find in the plants' growth across the three groups. She sees this as an opportunity to improve students' understanding

---

[12] Manz, E. (2015). Resistance and the development of scientific practice: Designing the mangle into science instruction. *Cognition and Instruction, 33*(2), 89–124.

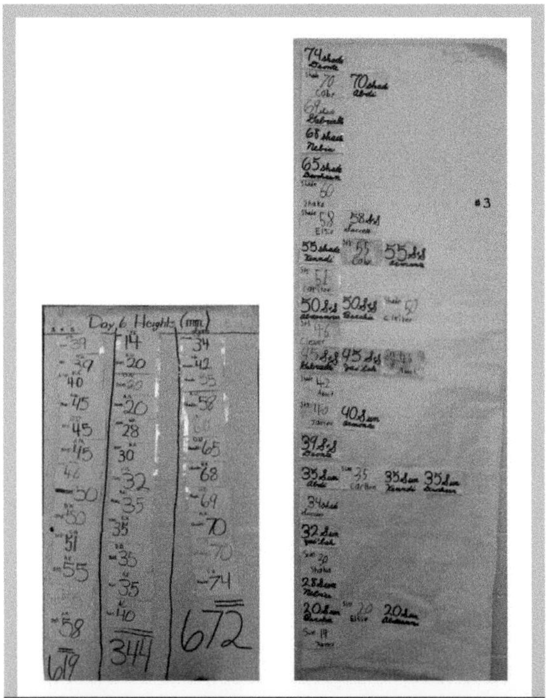

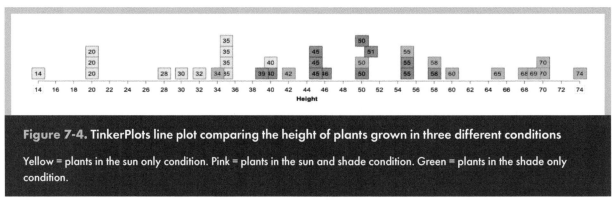

Figure 7-3. Two ways of displaying data on the height of plants grown in three different conditions

Source: Manz, 2015.

of data representations, and particularly of line plots, which are part of her state's third grade mathematics standards.

On day six of plant growth, Ms. Jafri asks the student to measure the heights of the plants in the three different conditions with a ruler and to record their data on index cards. Working in pairs, students decide how to organize and present their data. After they're finished, Ms. Jafri guides the class in reviewing the different approaches used by pairs of students to display their comparisons of plant height. She asks students to consider which type of display best allows them to quickly see that on day 6, the plants in the shade were taller, in general. Two types of displays are shown in Figure 7-3. Ms. Jafri also supports children as they come up with explanations for why the shade plants tend to be taller—because these plants put their energy toward trying to grow upward to reach the sun.

In addition, Ms. Jafri has the children use TinkerPlots software to create a line plot displaying the heights of the plants (Figure 7-4). The children examine the line plot to see what findings emerge and how these findings connect with the other ways used to display the same data.

Figure 7-4. TinkerPlots line plot comparing the height of plants grown in three different conditions

Yellow = plants in the sun only condition. Pink = plants in the sun and shade condition. Green = plants in the shade only condition.

Source: E. Manz, personal communication.

Don't feel compelled to do this all at once!

Integration of various academic subjects must be carefully designed and implemented to make better use of instructional time and to deepen understanding of learning targets in multiple subjects. It's fine—even recommended—to approach integration gradually. As long as the connections between subjects are purposeful and the instructional activities mutually support learning in each of targeted subjects, you're on the right track.

QUESTIONS FOR REFLECTION

- How are these examples similar to or different from the way I currently integrate science with other subjects?

- In what ways am I attending to the points of overlap in learning goals across subjects?

- How can I make the points of connection explicit for my students?

- How can I find ways to build ELA or mathematics interventions into the context of science learning so students have access to learning in all subjects?

- Is integration the best strategy for this situation?

Epilogue: Finding Your Own Sources of Support

Everyone involved in writing and producing this practitioners' guide, including the educators who have shared their experiences in its pages, has done so in hopes of inspiring and empowering you to try something new—or validating what you're already doing. Whether you're relatively new to the instructional approaches in this guide or are already putting some of them into action, you may still, at times, find this work to be challenging. The strategies described in this guide may call for different ways of interacting with students than what you're accustomed to. Remember, you don't have to do everything at once, and you can choose or adapt the strategies you think will work best for you and your students.

Every chapter of this guide has made the point in some way that students learn more deeply when they talk together, collaborate on investigations and design tasks, and jointly construct explanations and arguments. The same rationale applies to you. As you implement the strategies in the chapters, your greatest source of ideas, strength, and stamina is often your colleagues.

Whether through an established professional learning community, grade-level team meetings, informal sharing of ideas, or an online community, many educators who are competent and comfortable with three-dimensional strategies credit their colleagues as a main source of support.

One such teacher is Marian Hobbes Moore, a K–5 STEM instructional coach in an urban, Southeastern district and a leader of a districtwide STEM teacher learning community. Many teachers in her district, especially those who taught the early grades, were intimated by the prospect of managing this approach to instruction and letting children handle science and engineering materials, says Hobbes Moore. What helped a lot, she explained, was when the teachers worked as teams and shared ideas and materials through the teacher learning community.

The biggest thing that was the most beneficial for all of us was being able to collaborate—knowing that we could call somebody and say, "Hey, I want to do this; do you have any ideas?" . . . You don't have to be alone in doing this. And you shouldn't be intimidated to do it. Because it is doable, especially if you start on a small scale and then build up.[1]

So, join or organize a group of colleagues to study and try out the science and engineering instructional strategies described in this guide. Exchange ideas and materials—and successes and flops—with a team or even one trusted co-worker. If your school or district has a science resource person or coach, take advantage of all they can offer.

Remind yourself that you bring many assets to this work. The National Academies' *Framework*, guides like this one, professional learning providers, and other reliable sources can provide ideas from research and expert practitioners to enhance your instruction. But you know your students and your context. If you merge what these resources can offer with what you already know, it can have a powerful, positive impact on your students and on your own teaching.

Lastly, cultivate the joy and wonder, the brilliance and strengths, that exist in preschool and elementary students—and in yourself. Take a lesson from a teacher who seized a serendipitous moment to kindle children's curiosity. While her students were taking an online assessment, she noticed that one child kept glancing toward the windows. She followed his eyes and saw a fox walking up the hill outside the school:

I looked up at everybody and said, "Fox break!" And they all got up, went straight to the windows, and we're watching the fox walk across the hill . . . It was just this moment of awe in watching the animal in motion and having a talk—"What do you think it's doing?" . . . And so, wonder, right?[2]

So, rise and thrive with science. This is hard work; you can do it—and don't forget the fox breaks!

---

[1] Interview, Feb. 11, 2022.
[2] Interview, Jan. 12, 2022.

Biographical Sketches
of Consultants

JENN BROWN-WHALE serves as the Elementary Science Resource Teacher for the Howard County Public School System. This Maryland district consists of 42 elementary schools serving approximately 24,000 K–5 students. Brown-Whale's role is focused on three main charges: curriculum development, professional learning, and instructional coaching. Brown-Whale served as a fourth-grade classroom teacher, as well as a sixth-grade outdoor educator prior to entering their role at the district level. Brown-Whale was a member of the Achieve/WestEd Peer Review Panel for two years and continues to participate in and lead a variety of curriculum development and evaluation projects outside their school system responsibilities. They hold a B.S. in Counseling and Human Services from Stevenson University and a Master of Arts in Teaching from Towson University.

JEANANE CHARARA is a professional development provider and K–2 science coach with the SOLID Start research project at Michigan State University. She also is currently a peer reviewer on WestEd's NextGenScience Peer Review Panel and is an EQuIP Science Leader. Charara evaluates science curriculum and determines their alignment to the NGSS as well as provides professional development on how to use the EQuIO rubric. Charara also works as a NGSX Elementary Pathway Designer. She was previously an Elementary STEAM Coach for Dearborn Public Schools in Dearborn, Michigan, where she provided professional development to K–5 teachers and helped guide teacher pedagogies to more equitable science teaching practices and NGSS aligned instruction. Charara also coached K–5 teachers by providing them with support in the science classroom and allowing them opportunities to demonstrate effective science instruction. She has a strong interest in K–2 science and obtaining a better understanding of how science may look different at the early elementary level. She has formerly taught as an elementary teacher and was the Distance Learning

Coordinator at the Michigan Science Center. She served on the National Academies of Sciences, Engineering, and Medicine consensus committees that authored the report *Science and Engineering in PK through Elementary Grades: The Brilliance of Children and Strengths of Teachers* (2022). Charara has a Bachelor of Science in Elementary Education with a focus in integrated sciences from Wayne State University. She has also received an M.Ed. in education with an emphasis on teaching English as a second or foreign language from Spring Arbor University.

STACEY (GRUBER) VAN DER VEEN is the Founder and Lead Consultant of Leadership in Science, LLC. She has extensive experience designing and delivering professional development programs to support New Jersey school districts as they implement the Next Generation Science Standards. van der Veen spends much of her time in schools working elbow to elbow with teams of teachers as they implement the vision behind the NGSS in their classrooms. She also works closely with science coaches and administrators to help them deepen their skills to serve as instructional leaders in their districts. Before founding Leadership in Science, van der Veen was the Manager of Education Programs for the Merck Institute for Science Education (MISE), a nationally recognized nonprofit organization dedicated to improving science teaching and learning in public schools. She started her career teaching science and math at high schools in Newark, New Jersey, and New York City and has over 20 years of K–12 teaching and administrative experience in both public and private schools. She co-founded the Hoboken Charter School, one of the first cohort of schools chartered in New Jersey, where she served as Co-Principal and Child Study Team Coordinator. van der Veen earned her Ed.M. in secondary science education from the Harvard Graduate School of Education and her B.A. in biology from the University of Pennsylvania.

About the Author and Contributing Authors

Primary Author

NANCY KOBER is a freelance writer, editor, and consultant specializing in education, with extensive experience in translating research findings into plain language. She is the author of *Reaching Students: What Research Says about Effective Instruction in Undergraduate Science and Engineering* (2015) for the National Academies, and of numerous publications about topics ranging from standardized testing to student motivation. Formerly, she was an editor, writer, and analyst for the Center on Education Policy at the George Washington University and for GW's Graduate School of Education and Human Development. Earlier in her career, she served as a legislative specialist for an education subcommittee of the U.S. House of Representatives. Kober holds a bachelor's degree in English from Cornell University and a master's degree in writing from the University of Virginia.

Contributing Authors

HEIDI CARLONE is the Katherine Johnson Chair of Science Education in the Peabody College at Vanderbilt University. She was previously the Hooks Distinguished Professor of STEM Education in the Department of Teacher Education and Higher Education at The University of North Carolina at Greensboro. She is a teacher educator and educational researcher who works to make science and engineering pathways more accessible and equitable for historically underserved and underrepresented populations. Carlone's work leverages insights from research and practice. For example, insights from studying the culture of K–12 science and engineering learning settings allow her to co-develop design principles for equitable instruction, which then lead to a re-design and further study of the revised learning goals and activities. Her current work focuses on three primary questions: (1) How can innovative K–8 science and engineering instruction cultivate more meaningful and expansive learning outcomes (e.g., STEM identities) for diverse youth? (2) How can we enrich K–8 diverse youths' science and engineering learning ecologies in sustainable ways? (3) How can we design professional learning networks to support, nurture, and celebrate rigorous and equitable science and engineering teaching and retain excellent teachers in high needs schools? She has received a number of awards in her academic career, including the UNCG Alumni Teaching Excellence Award; the Early Career Research Award from the National Association for Research in Science Teaching; and the Early Career Development Award (CAREER) from the National Science Foundation. She served on the National Academies of Sciences, Engineering, and Medicine consensus committee that released the report *Science and Engineering in Preschool Through Elementary Grades: The Brilliance of Children and the Strengths of Educators* (2022). Carlone received her Ph.D. in instruction and curriculum from the University of Colorado, Boulder.

ELIZABETH A. (BETSY) DAVIS is a professor at the University of Michigan, School of Education. Her research focuses on beginning elementary teachers learning to engage in rigorous, consequential, equitable, and just science teaching, as well as the roles of curriculum materials and practice-based teacher education in promoting teacher learning. She was the chair for the Elementary Teacher Education Program at the University of Michigan for four years and helped lead the reshaping and redesign of this practice-based program. Davis received the Presidential Early Career Award for Scientists and Engineers at the White House in 2002. She has served on National Research Council committees focused on teacher learning and instructional materials, and chaired the National Academies of Sciences, Engineering, and Medicine committee that released the report *Science and Engineering in Preschool Through Elementary Grades: The Brilliance of Children and the Strengths of Educators*. Davis earned her Ph.D. in education in mathematics, science, and technology from the University of California, Berkeley.

XIMENA DOMÍNGUEZ is the executive director of learning sciences and early learning research at Digital Promise. Her research focuses on young children's STEM learning across home and school and involves partnerships with public preschool educators, curriculum developers, media designers and families from historically and systematically excluded communities to co-design equitable learning experiences for young children. In addition to studying how science, mathematics and engineering can be meaningfully promoted early in childhood, her current work investigates how STEM domains can be feasibly and meaningfully integrated in preschool classrooms. Across these efforts, she explores the affordances of technology and media for supporting early teaching and learning—documenting how digital tools can be designed to strengthen (not replace) the hands-on, socially rich, and collaborative learning that is key early in childhood. She currently leads Digital Promise's strategic effort on multilingual learners and recently served on the National Academies of Sciences, Engineering, and Medicine committee that released the report *Science and Engineering in Preschool Through Elementary Grades: The Brilliance of Children and the Strengths of Educators*. Her work has been funded by the National Science Foundation, the Institute of Education Sciences, and philanthropic foundations. Domínguez earned an M.S.Ed. in education from the University of Pennsylvania and a Ph.D. in applied developmental psychology from the University of Miami.

EVE MANZ is associate professor of science education at the Boston University Wheelock College of Education & Human Development. Her research focuses on understanding how to design and orchestrate learning environments that engage young students in science practices such as modeling, argumentation, and explanation. Manz works closely with elementary teachers and instructional leaders to develop approaches to science teaching and learning that center student and teacher sensemaking. This includes understanding elementary teaching and learning as part of a multi-content area system to better support classroom instruction within and across the content areas of science, ELA, and mathematics. She draws from her experience as an elementary school teacher and educational director of a science and engineering museum. Her work has been funded by the James S. McDonnell Foundation, the George Lucas Educational Foundation, and a CAREER grant from the National Science Foundation. She is the recipient of the 2019 Early Career Research Award from the National Association for Research in Science Teaching. She served on the National Academies of Sciences, Engineering, and Medicine consensus committee that released the report *Science and Engineering in Preschool Through Elementary Grades: The Brilliance of Children and the Strengths of Educators*. Manz received her Ph.D. in mathematics and science education from Vanderbilt University.

CARLA ZEMBAL-SAUL holds the Kahn Professorship in STEM Education at Penn State University where she has served in a number of leadership positions, including Department Head for Curriculum & Instruction and Co-coordinator of the Elementary and Early Childhood Education Program. She is a science teacher educator, educational researcher, biologist, and former middle school science teacher. Zembal-Saul's research and practice are situated in school–university–community partnerships; her work supports and investigates preservice and practicing K-5 teachers as they learn to engage students in equitable science sensemaking through investigation and design. Her most recent work is with public school teachers and afterschool educators who work with emergent multilingual children and their families in two semi-urban communities undergoing rapid demographic shifts. Zembal-Saul has been recognized for her scholarship, such as the National Science Teaching Association Fellow, Penn State Provost's Award for Collaboration, the National Science Foundation Early Career Development Award (CAREER), and the Kahn Professorship. She served on the National Academies of Sciences, Engineering, and Medicine consensus committees that authored the reports *Science Teachers' Learning: Enhancing Opportunities, Creating Supportive Contexts* (2015) and *Science and Engineering in Preschool through Elementary Grades: The Brilliance of Children and Strengths of Teachers*. Zembal-Saul earned her Ph.D. and B.S. in Science Education from The University of Michigan.

Acknowledgments

The development of this book was made possible through a grant provided by the Carnegie Corporation of New York. The ongoing support of Jim Short, program director of the Leadership and Teaching to Advance Learning portfolio within the Carnegie Corporation of New York, has been essential to the project. This book is based on the 2022 National Academies of Sciences, Engineering, and Medicine consensus report *Science and Engineering in Preschool through Elementary Grades: The Brilliance of Children and the Strengths of Educators*, which was supported by grants from the Carnegie Corporation of New York and the Robin Hood Learning + Technology Fund.

We are deeply grateful to the primary author, Nancy Kober, for her dedication and commitment to seeing this project through to completion despite several challenges. Her talent for speaking directly to teachers and bringing classrooms to life through her writing have made this book sing. We would also like to express gratitude to the contributing authors Heidi Carlone, Betsy Davis, Xime Dominguez, Eve Manz, and Carla Zembal-Saul. Their willingness to step up during a pivotal point in development of the book was essential. We extend a special thank you to Betsy and Xime, who have been involved throughout the full process, including the generation of the structure of the book and identification of potential examples and interviewees.

A group of expert practitioners and researchers in the field of elementary science education served as consultants and provided ongoing input in the development of this book. Their invaluable guidance throughout the process is acknowledged with appreciation. This group included Jenn Brown-Whale, Elementary Science Resource Teacher; Jeanane Charara, professional development provider and K-2 science coach; and Stacey van der Veen, Founder and Lead Consultant of Leadership in Science, LLC. Additional suggestions were provided throughout by Kendra R. Pullen, K-6 Science Curriculum Instructional Specialist, Caddo Parrish Public Schools.

We would also like to extend a special thank you to those individuals who participated in interviews with the primary author, Nancy Kober. Although many of the names have been anonymized, those interviews were crucial as they serve as the basis for many of the examples and guidance provided throughout this book.

Additional thanks are due to Audrey Webb, who provided insight into examples used in this guide through her practitioner lens as a former educator and state science lead. We also acknowledge the contributions of Margaret Kelly, who provided invaluable administrative support throughout the project as well as Brittani Shorter, who assisted in aspects of the work when needed. We would also like to extend a heartfelt thank you to Bea Porter, Kirsten Sampson-Snyder, and Anthony Janifer for helping to navigate the review process and the production of the book to include coordinating with the National Academies Press.

This Practitioner Guide was reviewed in draft form by individuals chosen for their diverse perspectives and technical expertise. The purpose of this independent review is to provide candid and critical comments that will assist the National Academies of Sciences, Engineering, and Medicine in making each published report as sound as possible and to ensure that it meets the institutional standards for quality, objectivity, evidence, and responsiveness to the study charge. The review comments and draft manuscript remain confidential to protect the integrity of the deliberative process.

We thank the following individuals for their review of this report:

Terrance Burgess, Michigan State University

Linda Cook, PK–12 Director of Science (retired), National Science Education Leadership Association (former president)

Amelia Wenk Gotwals, Michigan State University

Daryl Greenfield, University of Miami

Kendra R. Pullen, Caddo Parrish Public Schools

Enrique Suarez, University of Massachusetts at Amherst

The review of this report was overseen by Patricia Morison, National Academies. She was responsible for making certain that an independent examination of this report was carried out in accordance with the standards of the National Academies and that all review comments were carefully considered. Responsibility for the final content rests entirely with the authoring committee and the National Academies.

Finally, we want to acknowledge the members of the consensus committee that authored the *Brilliance and Strengths* report. Without their remarkable contributions, *Rise and Thrive with Science: Teaching PK–5 Science and Engineering* would not be a reality.

Amy Stephens, *Associate Director*
Heidi Schweingruber, *Director*
Board on Science Education